Surface
Works

Jenny Dowde

SALLYMILNER
PUBLISHING

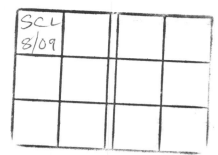

Dedication

To Chris and Paul—this one's for you

First published in 2007 by
Sally Milner Publishing Pty Ltd
734 Woodville Road
Binda NSW 2583 AUSTRALIA

© Jenny Dowde 2007

Design: Anna Warren, Warren Ventures Pty Ltd
Editing: Anne Savage
Photography: Tim Connolly

Printed in China

National Library of Australia Cataloguing-in-Publication data:

Dowde, Jenny.
 Surface works.

 ISBN 9781863513753 (pbk.).

 1. Knitting. 2. Crocheting. I. Title.
 (Series : Milner craft series).

746.43

Disclaimer
Information and instructions given in this book are presented in good faith, but no warranty is given nor results guaranteed, nor is freedom from any patent to be inferred. As we have no control over physical conditions surrounding application of information herein contained in this book, the author and publisher disclaim any liability for untoward results.

10 9 8 7 6 5 4 3 2 1

Contents

Acknowledgements

Writing a book is never a one-person accomplishment. Many people in so many ways contribute, some knowingly, some unknowingly, and once again I have many people to thank.

Firstly, huge thanks to Chris, my long-suffering husband, who has lived 'with the mess' since 2004 and put up with me through three books!

To Sue Bennett for doing the knitting thing—it helped more than you know.

To Gail McHugh for doing the pattern-writing thing—'technical' is definitely not my forte!

To my friends at the gym (including the Three Stooges—aka Mick, Dave and Tony)—your combined sense of humour has helped keep me sane through three books!

To my usual cheer squad—too many to list but you know who you are. Thanks for the support and encouragement.

To Ian and Libby of Sally Milner Publishing, who continue to support my writing efforts.

To the Design and Editorial Departments at Sally Milner Publishing, whose combined talents turn a duckling into such a beautiful swan.

To Judy Harris once again for the loan of her 'girls'.

A very special thanks to the following people who so generously donated the yarn used in this book: Jenny Bellew of Cleckheaton, Luisa Gelenter of La Lana Wools, JoAnne Turcot of Plymouth Yarns, and Anni Kristensen of Himalaya Yarn.

Thanks also to Barry Klein of Trendsetter Yarns for the paillettes.

All the garments in this book were designed using Garment Designer by Cochenille. www.cochenille.com

Introduction

I love strange choices. I'm always interested in people who depart from what is expected of them and go into new territory.

CATE BLANCHETT

Surface Works is about using plain knitted or crocheted backgrounds to which surface decoration can be added. As well as a host of smaller projects I have included instructions for several garments. Although these projects have been 'decorated' in particular ways, you don't have to use the same technique I did on any given item. There are many alternative meanings for *decorate*, including adorn, bedeck, brighten, do up, embellish, enhance, enrich, festoon, frill, gussy up, jazz up, ornament and trim, all of which illustrate the focus of the book and also mean you have the freedom to choose your own decorative technique or to combine several to create your own unique look.

One of advantages about this method of working is that most projects take only small amounts of those expensive fancy yarns which are constantly telling me to buy them—so you are guaranteed at least two items from the one purchase and sometimes even three.

Apart from fancy yarns there are many other options for decorating your work—shop-bought braids and trims, beads, buttons, lace inserts, which can all be purchased reasonably cheaply, and all kinds of 'found objects'. There are countless ways of using these items to create interesting surfaces. *Surface Works* treats some of them in a traditional way and others in a somewhat freeform manner.

There are three main categories of surface decoration:

Altering the surface This can be as simple as adding another thread to an existing one, as I did in the Sari Silk bag (see page 99).

Using basic stitches and fancy yarns will produce a richly textured surface and result in a much more interesting fabric with little effort on your part (see the Spiral Cushion, page 123).

Collaging (or layering the surface) This involves adding objects to the background, in combination or isolation—beads, lace, cloth, braids, knit and crocheted motifs, etc.

Interrupting the surface This entails working in a certain technique such as garter stitch or double crochet (single crochet) for a few centimetres (inches) and then introducing something different—for example, changing from knitting to crochet or from one stitch technique to another so that the surface appearance of the fabric changes.

The end results of working with these methods can be elaborately ornate, totally crazy or subtle and elegant.

As with my first two books, *Freeform Knitting and Crochet* and *FREEformations, Surface Works* is meant to be an ideas book, not necessarily a pattern book. By all means make the projects exactly as shown if you want but, more importantly, have fun and create your own masterpieces from the ideas given.

A final note: as a freeformer, I'm not completely comfortable working with tension swatches and correct gauges so only the garments were worked to a gauge to ensure proper fit. The other projects were created with more of a freeform approach, and I have supplied only the yarns and needle or hook size information. If you use what I've suggested, any resultant differences between your tension and mine will simply mean a slightly larger or smaller item and, in the spirit of this book, that won't be a problem.

Twenty years from now you will be more disappointed by the things you didn' t do than by the ones you did do. So throw off the bowlines. Sail away from the safe harbour. Catch the trade winds in your sails. Explore. Dream. Discover.

Mark Twain

Abbreviations

ch	chain
dc(sc)	double crochet(single crochet)
tr(dc)	treble (double crochet)
htr(hdc)	half treble(half double crochet)
dtr(tr)	double treble(treble)
tr tr(dtr)	triple treble(double treble)
dpn	double-pointed needles
inc	increase
dec	decrease
k2tog	knit 2 together
LH	left hand
RH	right hand
M1	make one
psso	pass slip stitch over
p2sso	pass 2 slip stitches over
RS	right side
WS	wrong side
rep	repeat
rem	remaining
sp	space
st st	stocking stitch
st(s)	stitch(stitches)
sl st	slip stitch
sl	slip
tbl	through back loop
yfwd	yarn forward
ybk	yarn back
yrh	yarn round hook
yon	yarn over needle
ytf	yarn to front (bring yarn between needles to front of work)

KNITTING NEEDLE EQUIVALENTS

Australia	USA
2 mm	0
2.5 mm	1
3 mm	2–3
3.5 mm	4
3.75 mm	5
4 mm	6
4.5 mm	7
5 mm	8
5.5 mm	9
6 mm	10
6.5 mm	10.5
7 mm	—
8 mm	11
9 mm	13
10 mm	15
12 mm	17
15 mm	19
20 mm	35

CROCHET HOOK EQUIVALENTS

Australia	USA
2 mm	B/1
2.5 mm	C/2
3 mm	D/3
3.5 mm	E/4
4 mm	F/5
4.5 mm	G/6
5 mm	H/8
5.5 mm	I/9
6 mm	K
7 mm	K/10.5

Textured Stitches

The stitches in this section can be used to interrupt the flow of a plain flat fabric or used as an allover pattern. Depending on the multiples of stitches required for any one pattern, you may need to temporarily add or deduct a few stitches in order to keep the pattern correct within the body of a garment. If this is necessary, don't forget to change things back to what they were once the pattern section is complete!

An even simpler way of 'interrupting the surface' is to use several different textured yarns, as in the Spiral cushion (see page 123).

CROCHETED RUCHING

Chain an even number of stitches and work a base row of any basic stitch. Change to a hook two sizes smaller than that being used for the item you are making.

*Beginning with 3 ch to count as the first tr(dc), work 2 tr(dc) into each stitch, ending with 1 tr(dc) in last stitch.

Work two more rows of tr(dc) without further increasing.

On the next row decrease to the original number of stitches as follows: make 3 ch to count as first tr(dc) and then work pairs of tr(dc) together (in other words you are decreasing), working 1 tr(dc) into last stitch.

Change back to the smaller hook and work three rows of tr(dc)*

Repeat the sequence from * to * for length required.

Fig 1 Crocheted ruching

3D TREBLES

Chain a multiple of 5 ch plus 3.

Base Row: 1 tr(dc) into 4th ch from hook, 1 tr(dc) into each ch to end, turn.

1st Row: (RS) 3 ch, miss first st, 1 tr(dc) into each st to end, turn.

2nd Row: As 1st row.

3rd Row: 1 ch, 1 sl st into first tr(dc), *miss next tr(dc), insert hook from front to back and from right to left, work 7 tr(dc) around stem of next tr(dc), insert hook from front to back and from left to right, work 7 tr(dc) around stem of next tr(dc), miss next tr(dc), sl st into next tr, rep from * ending with sl st into top of turning ch, turn.

4th Row: 3 ch, miss first sl st, *1 tr (dc) into each of the next 4 tr(dc) of 2nd row, 1 tr(dc) into next sl st of 3rd row, rep from * to end, turn.

Rows 1 to 4 form the pattern. Repeat as required.

Fig 2 3D trebles

BUMPS AND TRAILS

Worked over a multiple of 8 sts, plus 1 extra.

1st Row: (WS) p1, *k1, p1, k5, p1, rep from * to end of row.

2nd Row: k1, *p5, k1, p1, k1, rep from * to end of row.

3rd Row: p1, *k into loop between the st just worked and the next st on the LH needle (called M1), (k1, p1, k1) all into the next st, M1, p1, p5 tog, p1, rep from * to end.

4th, 6th and 8th Rows: k1, *p1, k1, p5, k1, rep from * to end of row.

5th and 7th Rows: p1, *k5, p1, k1, p1, rep from * to end of row.

9th Row: p1, *p5tog, p1, M1 (k1, p1, k1) all into next st, M1, p1, rep from * to end of row.

10th Row: As 2nd row.

11th Row: As 1st row.

12th Row: As 2nd row.

These 12 rows form the pattern.

Fig 3 Bumps and trails

SUNBURST CHECK
SPECIAL ABBREVIATIONS
Cr4F—cross4 front
Cr4B—cross4 back

Worked over a multiple of 12 sts plus 2 extra.

1st Row: (RS) k4, *p6, k6, rep from * ending last repeat with k4.

2nd Row: p4, *k6, p6, rep from * ending last repeat with p4.

3rd Row: k3, *sl next onto a cable needle and hold at front of work, p3, then k1 from the cable needle (called Cr4F), sl next 3 sts onto a cable needle and hold at back of work, k1, then p3 from the cable needle (called Cr4B), k4, rep from * ending last repeat with k3.

4th Row: p3, *k3, p2, k3, p4, rep from * ending last repeat with p3.

5th Row: k2, *Cr4F, k2, Cr4B, k2, rep from * to end of row.

6th Row: p2, *k3, p4, k3, p2, rep from * to end of row.

7th Row: k1, *Cr4F, k4, Cr4B, rep from * to last st, k1.

8th, 10th and 12th Rows: As 1st row.

9th and 11th Rows: As 2nd row.

13th Row: k1, *Cr4B, k4, Cr4F, rep from * to last st, k1.

14th Row: As 6th row.

15th Row: k2, *Cr4B, k2, Cr4F, k2, rep from * to end of row.

16th Row: As 4th row.

17th Row: k3, *Cr4B, Cr4F, k4, rep from * ending last rep with k3.

18th Row: As 2nd row.

19th Row: As 1st row.

20th Row: As 2nd row.

These 20 rows form the pattern.

Fig 4 Sunburst check

BIG BUBBLES

Worked over a multiple of 10 sts, plus 2 extra.

1st and 3rd Rows: (WS) p.

2nd Row: k.

4th Row: k1, *(k5, turn, p5, turn) 3 times, k10, rep from * to last st, k1.

5th Row: As 1st row.

6th Row: As 2nd row.

7th Row: As 3rd row.

8th Row: k6, *(k5, turn, p5, turn) 3 times, k10, rep from * ending the last rep with k6.

These 8 rows form the pattern.

Fig 5 Big bubbles

LITTLE BUBBLES
SPECIAL ABBREVIATION

M1—pick up loop between previously worked stitch and next stitch and knit it.

Worked over a multiple of 6 plus 2 sts.

Cast on required number of stitches.

1st Row: k1, *with yarn at back of work sl 3 p-wise, yfwd, p3, rep from * to last st, k1.

2nd Row: k1, *k3, yfwd, sl 3 p-wise, ybk, rep from * to last st, k1.

3rd Row: As 1st row.

4th Row: As 2nd row.

5th Row: k1, *M1, k3tog, M1, k3, rep from * to last st, k1.

6th Row: p.

7th Row: k1, *p3, ybk, sl 3 p-wise, fwd, rep from * to last st, k1 omitting yfwd before knitting last st.

8th Row: k1, *yfwd, sl 3 p-wise, ybk, k3, rep from * to last st, k1.

9th Row: As 7th row.

10th Row: As 8th row.

11th Row: k1, *k3, M1, k3tog, M1, rep from * to last st, k1.

12th Row: p.

These 12 rows form the pattern.

Fig 6 Little bubbles

BALL AND CHAIN STITCH

Worked over a multiple of 6 plus 2.

Row 1: p2, *k4 into one st (working alternately into front and back), p2, k1, p2*.

Row 2: *k2, p1, k2, k4 taking yarn round needle twice on each stitch*, k2.

Row 3: p2, *k4 slipping extra loops off needle, p2, k1, p2.

Row 4: As 2nd row.

Row 5: As 3rd row.

Row 6: *k2, p1, k2, p4 tog*, k2.

Row 7: p2, *k1, p2, k4 into one st, p2*.

Row 8: *k2, k4 taking yarn round needle twice on each stitch, k2, p1*, k2.

Row 9: p2, *k1, p2, k4 slipping extra loops off needle, p2*.

Row 10: As 8th row.

Row 11: As 9th row.

Row 12: *k2, p4 tog, k2, p1*, k2.

Repeat rows1 to 12 as required.

Fig 7 Ball and chain
stitch

KNITTED-IN TUFTS

Cut lengths of net, fabric, wool roving, lace or ribbon 25 cm (10 in) long and 2 cm (½ in) wide.

Work to the position of the first tuft.

Place the length of fabric between the needles, holding approximately 4 cm (1½ in) at the front of the work.

Hold the rest of the fabric at the back, together with the length of working yarn.

With fabric and working yarn held together, knit the next 3 to 5 sts, depending on how far apart you want the tufts to be.

Bring the fabric strip to the front of the work, trim the end if necessary, and continue using the working yarn only.

Fig 8a Knitted-in tufts

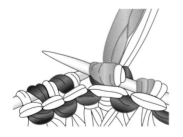

Fig 8b

Cord stitch

Can be worked over any number of stitches.

1st, 3rd, 5th and 7th Rows: (RS) k.

2nd, 4th and 6th Rows: p.

8th Row: k1, *pick up st in 4th row below the next st on LH needle and purl it tog with the next st on the LH needle, rep from * to last st, k1.

Fig 9 Cord stitch

Embossed rosebud

Worked over a multiple of 8 sts.

1st Row: *k3, p2, k3, rep from * to end.

2nd Row: *p3, sl next st onto a cable needle and hold at the from of the work, k1, yrn 5 times, then k1 from the cable needle, p3, rep from * to end.

3rd Row: k3, p1, k5 tbl, p1, k3, rep from * to end.

4th Row: *p3, (k1, yfwd) 6 times, k1, p3, rep from * to end.

5th Row: *k3, p13, k3, rep from * to end.

6th Row: *p3, k13, p3, rep from * to end.

7th Row: *k3, p2 tog, p9, p2 tog tbl, rep from * to end.

8th Row: *p3, sl 1, k1, psso, k7, k2tog, p3, rep from * to end.

9th Row: *k3, p2 tog, p5, p2 tog tbl, k3, rep from * to end.

10th Row: *p3, sl 1, k1, psso, k3, k2tog, p3, rep from * to end.

11th Row: *k3, p2 tog, p1, p2 tog tbl, k3, rep from * to end.

12th Row: *p3, sl 1, k1, psso, k1, p3, rep from * to end.

These 12 rows form the pattern.

Fig 10 Embossed rosebud

PICOT RIDGES

*Cast on 2 sts, cast off 3 sts, return remaining st on RH needle to the LH needle, rep from * to last st, cast on 2 sts, cast off 3 sts. Fasten off.

VERTICAL PICOT RIDGES

Pick up the bar of every 2nd row (if you gently pull the fabric sideways you will see the bars between each stitch).

DIAGONAL PICOT RIDGES

On a plain background pick up one half of each knit stitch diagonally across the face of the fabric and knit picots as before.

TIP If your background is to be stocking stitch and you have planned the position of your picots, you may like to work a row or part row of purl stitch where you want the picots to be to act as the base for picking up stitches. Pick up every second bump along the purl row. This will form the base row of stitches.

Fig 11a Vertical and diagonal picot ridges

CROCHET PICOT

For crocheted picots you can pick up directly from the background. Make a slip knot on hook, insert hook into fabric and draw yarn through. Work *1 dc(sc) into fabric, 3 ch, sl st back into first ch worked, dc(sc) in next loop of fabric. Repeat from * for distance required.

Fig 11b Crochet picot

QUILTED LATTICE

Worked over a multiple of 6 stitches plus 3 extra.

1st Row: (WS) p.

2nd Row: k2, *ytf, sl 5, k1, rep from * to last st, k1.

3rd Row: p.

4th Row: k4, *k the next st under the float of the 2nd row, k5, rep from * ending last rep with k4.

5th Row: p.

6th Row: k1, *ytf, sl 3, k1, ytf, sl 5, rep from * to last 5 sts, k1, ytf, sl 3, k1.

7th Row: p.

8th Row: k1, *k the next st under the float of the 6th row, k5, rep from * ending last rep k1.

Rows 1 to 8 form the pattern.

CROSS STITCH

Worked over an even number of stitches.

Cast on 20 sts and purl one row (or follow straight on from the stitch used for main fabric). This stitch will draw the fabric in width-wise, making it ideal for cuffs or hems where just a little narrowing is required.

1st Row: (RS) *put needle behind first st and knit into the back of 2nd st, then knit into the front of the first st, sl both sts off tog. Rep from * to end.

2nd Row: P1, *p 2nd st, then first st, and sl both sts off tog. Rep from * to end, p1.

Fig 13a Basic cross stitch

Fig 13b Cross stitch with stocking stitch

CROSS HONEYCOMB STITCH

This stitch can be a little tricky at first but do persevere with it as the end result is worth it. (See How To chapter for diagram on how to cross stitches.)

Worked over a multiple of 8 sts using 2 colours.

1st to 3rd Rows: With Col A, knit.

4th Row: With Col B, *sl 1 p-wise, p6 winding yarn 3 times around needle (that is, p1, wind yarn 3 times around needle for each stitch), sl 1 p-wise, rep from * to end of row.

5th Row: With Col B, *sl 1, sl next 6 sts on to RH needle dropping the extra loops, pass the 6 sts back onto the LH needle and k the 4th, 5th and 6th sts, then the 1st, 2nd, and 3rd sts, slipping them off the needle at the same time (called Cross 6), sl 1, rep from * to end of row.

6th Row: With Col A, p1, p6, *(p the sl st of the previous row, pushing the needle through the st and under the strands taken across back of work) twice, rep from * to last 7 sts, p 7.

7th, 8th and 9th Rows: With Col A, k.

10th Row: (you can introduce another colour here if you wish, otherwise proceed with Col B) With Col B, p3, *sl 2 p-wise, p6 winding yarn 3 times around needle after each st has been purled, rep from * to last 5 sts, sl 2 p-wise, p3.

11th Row: With B, k3, sl 2, Cross 6, rep from * to last 5 sts, sl 2, k3.

12th Row: With Col A, p3, *(p sl st of previous row, pushing needle through st and under the strands taken across back of work) twice, p6, rep from * to last 5 sts, p the sl sts as before, p 3.

These 12 rows form the pattern.

Fig 14 Cross honeycomb
stitch

BASIC KNIT BOBBLE

I'd never been all that keen on knitting bobbles until I started playing
with them for this book—and discovered they aren't so bad!

Look through your existing stitch patterns and imagine a bobble
included somewhere in that fabric. Think about using them at the base
of a lacy V, in vertical groups, in clusters, or place them randomly
whenever you feel like it.

Cast on 19 sts.

Knit 3 rows st st.

4th Row: *k4, (k1, p1, k1, p1, k1) all into same st, turn k5, turn, cast off
4 (bobble made), rep from * to last 4 sts, k4.

Knit a few rows st st and rep 4th row.

Fig 15 Basic knit bobble

BOXED BOBBLES

Worked over a multiple of 6 sts, plus 1 extra.

1st and 3rd Rows: (WS) p.

2nd Row: p.

4th Row: p1, *k5, p1, rep from * to end of row.

5th and 7th Rows: p.

6th Row: p1, *k2, (k1, yfd, k1) all into the next st, turn, k3, turn, p3, slip the 2nd and 3rd sts over 1st st on RH needle, k2, p1, rep from * to end of row.

8th Row: As 4th row.

These 8 rows form the pattern.

Sample shows fabric worked in one end of yarn over two pattern repeats and then doubled for one repeat.

Fig 16 Boxed bobbles

EYELET COLUMNS

Pattern is worked over a multiple of 13 sts.

1st Row: (RS) *k2, k2tog, yfwd, sl 1 k-wise, k1, psso, k1, k2tog, yfwd, sl 1 k-wise, k1, psso, k2, rep from * to end.

2nd Row: *p3, (p1, k1) into yfwd of previous row, p3, (p1, k1) into yfwd of previous row, p3, rep from * to end of row.

3rd Row: k.

4th Row: p.

These 4 rows form the pattern.

Fig 17 Eyelet columns; leave plain or thread ribbon through the holes

TUNISIAN KNITTING

I've only ever heard of Tunisian crochet so discovering this knit stitch was a pleasant surprise. It would make a great 'disruptive' stitch if used in narrow bands within plain fabric and is an excellent choice for cushions or bags.

For a sample, cast on 20 stitches and work two rows in st st.

3rd Row: Slip the first st k-wise, yfwd (making a stitch). Continue along the row, slipping one st and making one st, to the end of the row.

4th Row: Taking care not to lose the made stitch at the end of the first row, proceed as follows: knit the first 2 sts tog through the back of the loops. Continue knitting pairs of sts tog through the back of the loops to the end of the row.

Rows 3 and 4 form the pattern. Repeat for length required.

Adding a second colour creates a different look altogether and looks pretty good on the reverse side as well.

Fig 18a Tunisian knitting

Fig 18b Tunisian knitting
using two colours

FLUFFLE STITCH

For this stitch you need a fancy yarn that has gaps in it, such as Trendsetter's 'Checkmate' or Plymouth's 'Odyssey'. In fact any 'railroad track' yarn, or even a soft ribbon that is easily pierced, will work.

CROCHET FLUFFLE STITCH

Work a base row of ch to length required and one or more rows of dc(sc) to where you want the texture to commence.

On the next row, insert the hook into the first st and through the fancy yarn, draw yarn through and work st as normal. Repeat along row, spacing the fancy yarn at 2–3 cm (½–¾ in) intervals to form the fluffle effect.

KNIT FLUFFLE STITCH

Cast on required number of stitches and k one or more rows to where you want the texture to commence. Insert needle into first st and through fancy yarn, bring the point of the needle back through the fancy yarn and stitch, knit off as normal.

Repeat along row, spacing the fancy yarn at 2–3 cm (½–¾ in) intervals to form the fluffle effect.

Experiment with the spacing of this stitch, bearing in mind that long loops may catch on jewellery, door knobs and so forth.

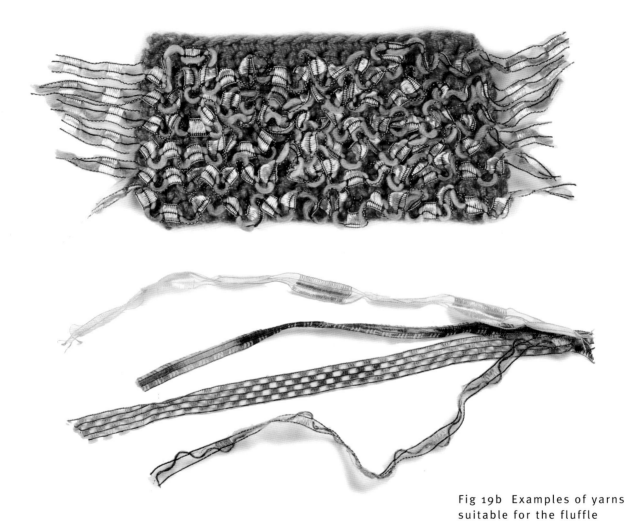

Fig 19a   Fluffle stitch

Fig 19b   Examples of yarns suitable for the fluffle stitch technique

To live a creative life, we must lose our fear of being wrong.

JOSEPH CHILTON PEARCE

Edgings and Inserts

Openwork and lacy edgings can be used to add length to a garment, to add interest to a plain fabric or, if made in fine yarn, used as an overlay. An allover patterned fabric can also be adapted for use as an edging or insert. Check out your own stitch pattern books for ideas.

SPIDER WEB FABRIC

Worked over a multiple of 14 ch plus 5 extra. A single repeat over 19 sts is ideal for a single motif that can be used as a collage element.

Make 19 ch.

Base Row: 1 tr(dc) into 4th ch from hook, tr(dc) into each st to end, turn.

1st Row: 3 ch [counts as first tr(dc)], 1 tr(dc) in next 2 tr, 5 ch, miss 2 tr, 1 dtr(tr) in next tr(dc), miss 2 tr, 1 dtr(tr) in next tr, miss 2 tr(dc), 1 dtr(tr) in next tr, 5 ch, 1 tr(dc) in last 3 tr, turn.

2rd Row: 3 ch, [counts as first tr(dc)], 1 tr(dc) in next 2 tr, 4 ch, 1 dc(sc) in last of 5 ch in previous row, 1 dc(sc) in top of next 3 sts, 1 dc(sc) in first of 5 ch in previous row, 1 tr(dc) in last 3 sts, turn.

3rd Row: 3 ch [counts as first tr(dc)], 1 tr(dc) in next 2 tr(dc), 5 ch, 1 dc(sc) in top of next 3 sts, 5 ch, 1 tr(dc) in last 3 sts, turn.

4th Row: 3 ch [counts as first tr(dc)], 1 tr(dc) in next 2 tr(dc), 2 ch, 1dtr(tr) in top of next 3sts, 2 ch, 1 tr(dc) in last 3 sts, turn.

5th Row: 3 ch [counts as first tr(dc)], 1 tr(dc) in next 2 tr(dc), *1 tr(dc) in each ch loop, 1 tr(dc) in next st, rep from * twice more, 1 tr(dc) in last 3 sts.

Fig 20 Spider web fabric

DROP LOOP EDGING

Worked over a multiple of 8 ch plus 2.

1st Row: (WS) 1 dc(sc) into 2nd ch from hook, 1 dc(sc) into each ch to end, turn.

2nd Row: 1 ch, 1 dc(sc) into next dc(sc), *3 ch, miss next 3 dc(sc), 3 tr(dc) into next dc(sc), turn, 5 ch, miss 2 tr(dc), sl st into next tr(dc), turn, 1 ch, 7 dc(sc) into next 5 ch sp, 3 ch, miss next 3 dc(sc), 1 dc(sc) into next dc(sc), rep from * to end. Fasten off.

Fig 21 Drop loop edging

Garter stitch points

You need to establish the number of stitches your garment requires before starting, and knit enough points to fit that number of stitches. Each point is made separately and knitted together at the end.

Cast on 2 sts.

1st Row: k2.

2nd Row: yfwd, k2.

3rd Row: yfwd, k to end.

Rep the 3rd row until the point is the required depth. Do not cast off. Break off yarn.

On the same needle make as many points as will fit the edge of your project. If you need more room than this, put some of the points on a stitch holder.

To complete the edging, knit across each point until all points have been joined. Continue knitting in your required fabric or cast off and sew the edging to the garment.

Fig 22 Garter stitch points

Stepped edging

This edging is worked sideways.

Cast on 6 sts.

1st, 2nd and 3rd Rows: k.

4th Row: Cast on 3 sts, k to end.

5th, 6th and 7th Rows: k.

8th Row: Cast on 3 sts, k to end.

9th, 11th, 13th, 14th and 15th Rows: k.

10th and 12th Rows: p.

16th Row: Cast off 3 sts, k to end.

17th, 18th and 19th Rows: k.

20th Row: Cast off 3 sts, k to end.

These 20 rows form the pattern repeat.

Fig 23 Stepped edging

SHELLS AND ARCHES

Worked over a multiple of 8 ch plus 5 extra.

Base Row: [2 tr(dc), 1 ch, 2 tr(dc)] into 9th ch from hook, *2 ch, miss 3 ch, 1 tr(dc) into next ch, 2 ch, miss 3 ch, [2 tr(dc), 1 ch, 2 tr(dc)] into next ch, rep from * to last 4 ch, 2 ch, miss 3 ch, 1 tr(dc) into last ch, turn.

Pattern Row: 5 ch, *[2 tr(dc), 1 ch, 2 tr(dc)] into next 1 ch sp, 2 ch, 1 tr(dc) into next tr(dc), 2 ch, rep from * to last shell group, [2 tr(dc), 1 ch, 1 tr(dc) into last 1 ch sp, 2 ch, miss first 2 turning ch, 1 tr(dc) into next ch, turn.

Repeat pattern row as required.

Fig 24 Shells and arches

LEAF EDGING

SPECIAL ABBREVIATION

y2rn—bring yarn forward and over the needle, then forward and over the needle again to make 2 sts.

Cast on 10 sts.

1st Row: k3, (yfwd, k2tog) twice, y2rn, k2tog, k1.

2nd Row: k3, p1, k2, (yfwd, k2tog) twice, k1.

3rd Row: k3, (yfwd, k2tog) twice, k1, y2rn, k2tog, k1.

4th Row: k3, p1, k3, (yfwd, k2tog) twice, k1.

5th Row: k3, (yfwd, k2tog) twice, k2, y2rn, k2tog, k1.

6th Row: k3, p1, k4, (yfwd, k2tog) twice, k1.

7th Row: k3, (yfwd, k2tog) twice, k6.

8th Row: Cast off 3 sts, k4, (yfwd, k2tog) twice, k1.

Fig 25 Leaf edging

PEAKED EDGING

Make 5 ch.

1st Row: Miss 3 ch, 4 tr(dc) in 4th ch, 2 ch, 1 dc(sc) in last ch, turn.

2nd Row: 3 ch, 4 tr(dc) in 2ch sp of previous row, 2 ch, 1 dc(sc) in 1st tr(dc) of group.

Rep 2nd row for required length.

Work side edge as follows:

1st Row: 3 ch, *1 dc(sc) in 3rd ch at beg of each motif, 3 ch*, rep from * to * along side edge.

2nd Row: Work 1 dc(sc) in dc(sc) of previous row and 3 dc in each 3ch sp.

Fig 26 Peaked edging

MESH LOOP EDGING

Make 13 sts.

1st Row: 1 tr(dc) in 4th ch from hook, 1 tr(dc) in next 2 ch, *1 ch, miss 1 ch, 1 tr(dc) in next ch, rep from * to end of row.

2nd Row: 8 ch, 1 tr(dc) in first 1 tr(dc), [1 ch, 1 tr(dc) in next 1 tr(dc)] 3 times, 1 ch, 1 tr(dc) in next 2 sts, 1 tr(dc) in 3rd of turning ch, turn.

3rd Row: 3 ch, 1 tr(dc) in next 2 sts, *1 ch, 1 tr(dc) in next st, rep from * to end, turn.

4th Row: 8 ch, 1 tr(dc) in first st, [1 ch, 1 tr(dc) in next 1 tr(dc)] 3 times, 1 ch, 1 tr(dc) in next 2 sts, 1 tr(dc) in 3rd of turning ch.

Rep rows 3 and 4 for required length.

Fig 27 Mesh loop edging

OCTOPUS FRINGE

Cast on 26 sts and knit 2 rows.

3rd Row: Cast off 22 sts, k to end.

4th Row: k4, cast on 22 sts, knit 2 rows on these 26 sts.

7th Row: Cast off 22 sts, k to end.

Repeat rows 4 to 7 for length required.

Fig 28 Octopus fringe

PICOT LOOP EDGING

Worked over a multiple of 5 sts.

Cast on required number of stitches.

1st Row: Knit.

2nd Row: Cast off first 2 sts, *slip rem st from RH needle onto LH needle, (cast on 2 sts, cast off next 2 sts, slip rem st onto LH needle) 3 times, cast on 2 sts, cast off 6 sts, rep from * to end. Fasten off.

Fig 29 Picot loop edging

TINY PICOTS

Work over a multiple of 5 sts.

*Insert the RH needle into the first st on the LH needle, cast on 2 sts, cast off 4 sts, slip the RH loop back onto LH needle (picot formed).

Repeat from * to end of row.

Experiment with this technique to create your own individual picot point edgings.

Fig 30a Tiny picots

Fig 30b Picot variations

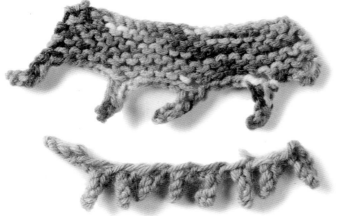

TRIPLE LOOP DROP
SPECIAL ABBREVIATION

triple loop—sl st into next dc(sc), (7 ch, 1 sl st) 3 times into same dc(sc).

Worked over a multiple of 8 sts plus 2 extra.

1st Row: (WS) work 1 dc(sc) into 2nd ch from hook, 1 dc(sc) into each ch to end, turn.

2nd Row: 1 ch, 1 dc(sc) into each dc(sc) to end, turn.

3rd Row: 1 ch, 1 dc(sc) into each of first 3dc, *9 ch, miss 3 dc(sc), 1 dc(sc) into each of next 5 dc(sc), rep from * to end omitting 2 dc(sc) at end of last rep, turn.

4th Row: 1 ch, 1 dc(sc) into each of first 2 dc(sc), *5 ch, 1 dc(sc) into next 9ch arch, 5 ch, miss 1 dc(sc), 1 dc(sc) into each of next 3 dc(sc), rep from * to end omitting 1 dc(sc) at end of last rep, turn.

5th Row: 1 ch, 1 dc(sc) into first dc(sc), *5 ch, miss 1 dc(sc), 1 dc(sc) into next dc(sc), rep from * to end, turn.

6th Row: 1 ch, 1 dc(sc) into first dc(sc), *5 ch, work 1 triple loop into next dc(sc), 5 ch, 1 dc(sc) into next dc(sc), rep from * to end. Fasten off.

Fig 31 Triple loop drop

RIBBON EYELET

Use this as an edging or insert.

Pattern is worked over an even number of stitches.

1st and 2nd Rows: k.

3rd Row: (RS) p1, *yrn, p2tog, rep from * to last st, p1.

4th, 5th, 7th and 8th Rows: k.

6th Row: p.

9th Row: p1, *yrn, p2tog, rep from * to end of row.

10th, 11th and 12th Rows: k.

These 12 rows form the pattern.

Variation: Thread ribbon or fancy yarn through the eyelets.

Fig 32   Ribbon eyelet

The creation of something new is not accomplished by the intellect but by the play instinct acting from inner necessity. The creative mind plays with the objects it loves.

CARL JUNG

Braids and Cords

TWISTED BRAID USING TWO COLOURS

Make 4 ch using Yarn A.

Base Row: 1 tr(dc) in 4th ch from hook, turn, *4ch, 1 tr(dc) in sp between tr(dc) and ch, turn, rep from * for length required. Fasten off.

1st Row: Using Yarn B and working into one edge of the base row, sl st in first sp at end of base row, *4ch, remove hook from loop, insert in next sp on base and pick up dropped loop, rep from * to end. Fasten off.

2nd Row: Work as for 1st row, working into the other side of the base row. Fasten off.

Fig 33 Twisted braid using two colours

SMALL FANCY BRAID

*Make 3 ch; in first ch work 1 htr(hdc), 1 tr(dc) and 1 dtr(tr). Rep from * for length required.

Fig 34 Small fancy braid

SHELL BRAID

Make 3 ch

1st Row: [3 tr(dc), 3 ch, 3 tr(dc)] into 3rd ch from hook, turn.

2nd Row: 3 ch, [3 tr(dc), 3 ch, 3 tr(dc)] into 3ch sp of previous row, turn.

Rep 2nd row for length required.

Leave as is or thread fancy yarn or ribbon through centre of the braid.

Fig 35   Shell braid

Fig 36   Lucet cords

LUCET CORDS

A lucet is a Y-shaped tool, usually made of wood, that makes square braids or cords as opposed to the round I-cord.

You can use whatever threads and fibres you like to make fine cords or heavy cords. They can be used for bag handles, necklaces, bracelets or surface decoration.

See the Toys of the Trade chapter for instructions on how to use a lucet and Resources for where to find one.

FAN BRAID

Worked over a multiple of 4 ch plus 1 extra.

1st Row: Miss 1 ch, 1 dc(sc) in each ch to end, turn.

2nd Row: *4 ch, 3 dtr(tr) in first of these 4 ch, miss 3 dc(sc), 1 dc(sc) in next dc(sc), rep from * to end.

Fig 37 Fan braid

SIDE-TO-SIDE BRAID

Make 5 ch and work 9 rows of dc.

10th Row: Working on side edge and into row 5, work [2 ch, 1 dtr(tr)] 5 times, 1 ch, sl st into row 1.

Turn work and into each 2ch sp work [1 dc(sc), 3 ch, 1 dc(sc)].

Rep these 10 rows, working the motifs on alternate side edges.

Fig 38 Side-to-side braid

BASIC HAIRPIN LOOM BRAIDS

The braids in Fig 39 were made on various sized looms using the basic technique as shown in the Toys of the Trade chapter.

There is a good range of different sized fixed looms available, or you can use an adjustable one (see Resources).

Fig 39 Basic hairpin loom braids

Fig 40 Twisted cord

For fancier braids try adding beads to the thread before making the braid, layer two braids together, and experiment with ribbons and other fibres not normally used for this technique. Fine gauge wire works well too.

TWISTED CORD

Take several long strands of yarn plus a fancy yarn such as an eyelash yarn, and make a twisted cord (see How To chapter).

This kind of cord is usually twisted tightly to make a firm, non-stretchy cord. If you want a softer effect you will need to stop twisting before it becomes too tight.

Colour Knitting
Without the Pain

I'm not very good with stranded colour knitting as I seem to have too many thumbs, so I like to use slipstitch patterns where only one colour is used at a time. There are lots of these patterns in stitch collection books so I've included just a few here. Experiment with the yarns you use for a different look. For instance if you use a chunky yarn with an 8-ply (DK), the resultant tweedy texture is quite unique. Try using needles a couple of sizes bigger that you normally would for the yarn used.

FINGERTIP TWEED
Worked over a multiple of 4 sts plus 3 extra, and uses 3 colours referred to as Col A, Col B and Col C.

Using Col C, cast on required number of sts.

1st Row: (RS) Using Col A, k3, *sl 2nd st on LH needle over first st and onto RH needle, k3, rep from * to end.

2nd Row: Using Col A, p3, *sl 1 p-wise, p3, rep from * to end.

3rd Row: Using Col B, k1, *sl 2nd st on LH needle over first st and onto RH needle, k3, rep from * to last 2 sts, k2.

4th Row: Using Col B, p1, *sl p-wise, p3, rep from * to last 2 sts, sl 1 p-wise, p1.

5th and 6th Rows: Using Col C, rep 1st and 2nd rows.

7th and 8th Rows: Using Col A, rep 3rd and 4th rows.

9th and 10th Rows: Using Col B, rep 1st and 2nd rows.

11th and 12th Rows: Using Col C, rep 3rd and 4th rows.

Fig 41 Fingertip tweed

STAR TWEED IN TWO COLOURS

Worked over a multiple of 4 sts plus 1 extra.

1st Row: Using Col B, cast on required number of sts and purl one row.

2nd Row: (RS) Using Col A, k1, *sl 1 p-wise, yon, sl 1 p-wise, k1, pass first sl st over last 3 sts, k1, rep from * to end.

3rd Row: Using Col A, p to end.

4th Row: Using Col B, k3, *sl 1 p-wise, yon, sl 1 p-wise, k1, pass first sl st over last 3 sts, k1, rep from * to last 2 sts, k2.

5th Row: Using Col B, p to end.

Rows 2 to 5 form the pattern.

Fig 42 Star tweed in two colours

THREE-COLOUR WAFFLE

Worked over a multiple of 10 sts plus 5 extra.

SPECIAL NOTE

Slip all sl sts with yarn on wrong side of fabric.

1st Row: (RS) Using Col A, k to end.

2nd Row: Using Col A, (p1, k1) twice, *p1, k1, p1, k1, rep from * to last 6 sts, p2, (k1, p1) twice.

3rd Row: Using Col B, k5, *(sl 1, k1) twice, sl 1, k5, rep from * to end.

4th Row: Using Col B, k5, *(sl 1, k1) twice, sl 1, k5, rep from * to end.

5th Row: Using Col A, k.

6th Row: Using Col A, k5, *(p1, k1) twice, p1, k5, rep from * to end.

7th to 10th Rows: As 3rd to 6th rows.

11th and 12th Rows: As 3rd and 4th rows.

13th and 14th Rows: As 1st and 2nd rows.

15th Row: Using Col C, (sl 1, k1) twice, sl 1, *k5, (sl 1, k1) twice, sl 1, rep from * to end.

16th Row: Using Col C, (sl 1, k1) twice, sl 1, *k5, (sl 1, k1) twice, sl 1, rep from * to end.

17th Row: As 5th row.

18th Row: Using Col A, (p1, k1) twice, p1, *k5, (p1, k1) twice, p1, rep from * to end.

19th and 20th Rows: As 15th and 16th rows.

21st Row: As 5th row.

22nd Row: As 18th row.

23rd Row: As 15th row.

24th Row: As 16th row.

These 24 rows form the pattern.

Fig 43 Three-colour
waffle

WINDOWBOXES

Worked over a multiple of 4 sts plus 3 extra.

The sample uses 2 colours, with Col B being a variegated yarn, but you can use 3 colours if you like, introducing the 3rd colour at the 5th row.

SPECIAL NOTE

Slip all sl sts with yarn on wrong side of fabric.

1st Row: (RS) With Col A, k.

2nd Row: Using Col A, k1, *k1 winding yarn twice around needle, k3, rep from * ending last rep with k1 instead of k3.

3rd Row: Using Col B, k1, drop extra loops then sl 1, k3, rep from * ending last rep with k1 instead of k3.

4th Row: Using Col B, k1, *sl 1, k3, rep from * to last 2 sts, sl 1, k1.

5th Row: Using Col A, k1, *sl 2, k2, rep from * to last 2 sts, sl, k1.

6th Row: Using Col A, k1, sl 1, *p2, sl 2, rep from * to last st, k1.

These 6 rows form the pattern repeat.

Fig 44 Windowboxes

VERTICAL STRIPES IN TWO COLOURS
Requires a multiple of 4 sts plus 3 extra.

1st Row: Using Col A, k to end.

2nd Row: Using Col A, p to end.

3rd Row: Using Col B, k3, *sl 1, k3, rep from * to end.

4th Row: Using Col B, p3, *sl 1, p3, rep from * to end.

5th Row: Using Col A, k1, *sl 1, k3, rep from * to last 2 sts, sl 1, k1.

6th Row: Using Col A, p1, *sl 1, p3, rep from * to last 2 sts, sl, p1.

Repeat 3rd to 6th rows for pattern.

Fig 45 Vertical stripes in
two colours

Collage

This technique can be considered as layering or creating an assemblage on the surface of your fabric as defined below.

collaging a: An artistic composition of materials and objects pasted over surface, often with unifying lines and color. b: An assemblage of diverse elements.

assemblage A sculptural technique of organising or composing into a unified whole a group of unrelated and often fragmentary or discarded objects.

(WWW.DICTIONARY.COM)

Among the many possibilities for collage are beads, buttons, bits of interesting fabric, felt cut into shapes, loosely knitted or crocheted overlays, shells, paper clips, tiny brass washers from the hardware store, rubber O-rings, shop-bought braids and ribbons, knitted or crocheted braids, old costume jewellery found at thrift shops, lace, feathers and commercial trims, to name a few. If you don't already have a collection of suitable objects lying around your studio, then give yourself a day off from your usual routine to wander around the craft shops, hardware stores, second-hand shops and thrift shops in your area. And don't forget to have a leisurely lunch as an extra treat!

Another good source of collage elements is knitted and crocheted inserts and edgings that instead of being used for their intended purpose can be overlaid on a plain background.

Very special 'found objects', which found their way to me courtesy of Luisa Gelenter, are spun fibres from her La Lana Wools range called 'Stone Soup' and 'Jewels', which I used as trimming on the Walnut vest and Sue's hat (see pages 171 and 117).

Another very special 'found object' was sent to me by Barry Klein of Trendsetter Yarns. They are crinkled 'paillettes' in a variety of shapes and sizes, including ovals, squares, rounds and boxes. I've used ovals and rounds in the Spangles necklace (see page 140).

Fig 46 Collection of found objects

Knitted and crocheted flowers are traditionally one of the easiest and most popular ways to decorate your garments and accessories. You will find lots of these in your collections of magazines and books but I've included a few 'new to me' basic patterns here for you to enjoy as well. It's fun to change the instructions a little or to add beads or other 'bits' to create your own unique look.

PICOT FLOWER

SPECIAL ABBREVIATION
inc 1—increase 1

Place a slipknot loop onto LH needle and *cast on 3 sts, cast off 3 sts, return the rem loop to LH needle. Rep from * 5 times.

Join points into flower by picking up and knitting a stitch through the original slipknot loop. Cast off 1 st, transfer rem loop to LH needle.

MAKE PETAL
*Cast on 1 st.

1st Row: k1, work into back, then into front of next st (called inc 1).

2nd, 4th, 6th, 7th, 8th, 9th, 11th, 13th and 15th Rows: knit.

3rd Row: k2, inc 1.

5th Row: k3, inc 1 (5 sts).

10th, 12th and 14th Rows: k2tog, k to end.

16th Row: k2tog*

With RH needle knit up 1 st between first and 2nd picot points. Cast off 1 st. Transfer loop to LH needle. Rep from * to * 5 times (6 petals).

Fig 47 Picot flower

LARGE FLOWER #1

This flower measures approximately 8 cm (3½ in) in diameter when worked in 8-ply yarn with 4 mm (F/5) hook. Use finer yarn for a smaller version

Make 6 ch, join with a sl st to form a circle.

1st Round: 3 ch, 2 tr(dc) into circle, [7 ch, 3 tr(dc) into circle)] 4 times, 7 ch, 1 sl st into 3rd of 3 ch.

2nd Round: 3 ch, [miss 1 tr(dc), 1 tr(dc) into next tr(dc), 15 dtr(tr) into 7ch loop, 1 tr(dc) into next tr(dc)] 4 times, miss 1 tr(dc), 1 tr(dc) in next tr(dc), 15 dtr(tr) in 7ch loop, sl st to top of 3 ch. Fasten off.

Fig 48 Large flower #1

LARGE FLOWER #2

This flower measures approximately 10 cm (4 in) when worked in 8-ply yarn with 4 mm (F/5) hook.

Make 8 ch, join with sl st to form a circle.

1st Round: 12 dc(sc) into circle, 1 sl st into first dc(sc).

FIRST PETAL

1st Row: 2 dc(sc) into same place as sl st, 2 dc(sc) into next dc(sc), 3 ch, turn.

2nd Row: Miss first dc(sc), 1 tr(dc) into each of next 3 dc(sc), 3 ch, turn.

3rd Row: 2 tr(dc) into first tr(dc), 3 tr(dc) into each of next 2 tr(dc), 3 tr(dc) into top of turning ch, 3 ch, turn.

4th and 5th Rows: Miss first tr(dc), 1 tr(dc) into each tr(dc) and into top of turning ch, 3 ch, turn (4 ch at end of 5th row).

6th Row: Miss first tr(dc), leaving last loop of each on hook, work 4 dtr(tr) over next 4 tr(dc), yarn over and draw through all loops on hook (cluster made), 4 ch, 1 dc(sc) into each of next 2 tr(dc), 4 ch, work a 4 dtr(tr) cluster over next 4 tr(dc), 4 ch, 1 sl st into top of turning ch, sl st down side of petal and sl st to next dc(sc) on circle.

Make 4 more petals in same way, ending last petal with sl st into dc(sc) at base of petal.

Fig 49 Large flower #2

TINY FLOWER

The samples were worked in a fine 2-ply yarn and #4 crochet cotton

Make 5 ch, join with sl st to form a circle.

1st Round: 1 ch, 12 dc(sc) into circle, sl st into first ch.

2nd Round: *Miss next dc(sc), 5 tr(dc) into next dc(sc), miss next dc(sc), sl st into next dc(sc), rep from * twice. Fasten off.

Fig 50 Tiny flower

FIVE-PETAL FLOWER

1st Round: Make 4 ch, join with a sl st to form ring.

2nd Round: (RS) [4 ch, 3 dtr(tr), 4 ch, sl st] into ring 5 times. Fasten off.

To make a four-petal flower work the 2nd round repeating the instructions inside the brackets 4 times instead of 5.

Fig 51 Five-petal flower

Fig 52 Four-petal flower

FLUFFLE FLOWER

See instructions for fluffle stitch in the Textured Stitches chapter.

You will need a fancy yarn with gaps, like a railway track yarn, or a yarn that has two different threads that are joined every few centimetres or so, or a ribbon yarn that is easily pierced by a crochet hook.

Make 4 ch, join with sl st into a circle

1st Round: Working in fluffle st work 8 dc(sc) into circle, join with sl st to first dc(sc) in round.

2nd Round: Work another round of fluffle st while working 2 dc(sc) into each st of previous round, join with sl st to first dc(sc) in round.

3rd Round: Work one round of tr(dc) increasing in every 2nd dc(sc), join with sl st to first tr(dc) in round.

4th Round: 3 ch, 1 dc(sc) in same place as sl st, *1 dc(sc), 3 ch, 1 dc(sc) in next st, rep from * around circle, ending with sl st at base of first dc(sc) in round. Fasten off.

Fig 53 Fluffle flower

SEVEN

My friend Cris Boerner invented this cute flower during a workshop we were attending at the Geelong Fibre Forum here in Australia and graciously gave me permission to share it with you.

You can use 12-ply (bulky) yarn for the outer and 8-ply (DK) for the inner section with a 4.5 mm (US7) crochet hook, 8-ply for both inner and outer sections with a 4.5 mm hook, or 5-ply (Sport Weight) for both outer and inner sections with a 3 mm (US2) hook. It's a fun flower to experiment with.

OUTER SECTION

Special stitch

Cluster—leaving last loop of each st on hook, work 4 tr(dc) into circle, yrh and draw through all 5 loops on hook (cluster made).

1st Round: 3 ch, work 13 tr(dc) in first ch, join with sl st into first tr(dc).

2nd Round: Work dc(sc) in same place as sl st, *4 tr(dc) cluster in next st, sl st into base of cluster, dc(sc) in next st, rep from * 6 times, 4 tr(dc) cluster in next st, sl st into base of cluster, sl st into first dc(sc) in round. Fasten off.

INNER SECTION

2 ch, 7 or 8 dc(sc) into first ch, join with sl st into first dc(sc) Fasten off.

ASSEMBLY

Place the inner section into the centre of the outer section and stitch into place. Sew beads into centre of flower if desired.

Fig 54 Seven

PAPER CLIPS

1st Row: Work a base row of dc(sc), htr(hdc) or tr(dc), 1 ch, turn.

2nd Row: Work in dc(sc) to where you want your first paper clip to sit.

Place paper clip onto hook, insert hook into next st and work 1 dc(sc) as normal, dc(sc) to next position. For hanging clips that's all you need to do.

For attached clips, as in the samples, continue as follows:

3rd Row: Work enough rows of dc(sc) so that the top of the paper clip, when flipped upwards, is almost level with the last row worked—it's OK if you find yourself on the wrong side of the fabric. You will just need to insert your hook into the fabric first. Insert hook into the top of the clip, then into the stitch behind the clip and work a dc(sc) as normal.

For the zigzag sample, work a few rows of dc(sc), *attach a clip, miss 5 dc(sc), attach two clips in next two stitches, miss 5 dc(sc), rep from * across row.

To attach the top of the clips, work 3 rows of dc(sc).

Next row: Work 4 dc(sc), attach a clip in next 2 sts, *miss 6 dc(sc), attach a clip in next 2 sts, rep from * across row.

Fig 55 Vertical paper clips

Fig 56 Zigzag paper clips

FABRIC FRAGMENTS

Using fabric fragments in collage is a little more time-consuming than a lot of the other techniques in this book, but fun and very effective nonetheless.

I've used organza in the sample because it's 'crisp', easy to rip and doesn't fray to within an inch of its life. Investigate the possibilities, as I'm sure there are many other fabrics that will work just as well.

Tear the fabric into 2.5 cm (1 in) wide strips and then roughly cut them into 2.5 cm (1 in) squares. They don't need to be exact, and look better if they aren't!

Using a strong thread, randomly stitch the squares onto the area you want to decorate, crowding them up as much as you can to create a richly textured surface. If you like you can add beads as you go or go back later and sew them on.

Fig 57 Organza fabric fragments

Felt shapes

Another nice idea is to use shapes cut from craft felt or from 'real' felt you've made yourself or purchased. The Basic Crocheted hat (see page 112) is trimmed with flowers cut from felt sheets which were sent to me by La Lana Wools, but you could use geometric shapes if you prefer.

Fig 58 Felt shapes

EMBROIDERY

Simple embroidery is an easy way of adding interest to a garment. It works well for pockets or collars or you can embroider directly onto the garment itself.

Fig 59 shows crocheted fabric decorated with cross-stitch, diagonally wrapped stitches, chain stitch and simple weaving using yarn.

Fig 59 A variety of embroidery stitches adds interest here

ATTACHED SURFACE CORDS

Here you can use I-cords, or crocheted chain lengths knitted or crocheted in as you work ...

Fig 60 Knitted in crocheted chain length

CROCHETED AND KNIT COLLAGE ELEMENTS

Apart from some of the braid and edging ideas already introduced, there are many motifs that would be suitable for collage work. They can be used on garments, on bags and hats, on the ends of scarves and on rugs or throws. Make them in fine crochet or embroidery threads or use a lightweight yarn. Use chunky yarns if you like, although the end result will be quite bulky.

For a little extra bling, add Lurex to a plain yarn, or knit or crochet with beads as you work.

CHAIN SPACE TRIANGLE

Wind yarn once around first finger (this method of working allows you to close the circle a little).

1st Round: 1 ch, 6 dc(sc) into circle formed on finger, sl st to first ch.

2nd Round: 10 ch, miss first dc, *tr(dc) into next dc(sc), 3 ch, 1 tr(dc) into next dc(sc), 7 ch, rep from * once more, 1 tr(dc) into next dc(sc), 3 ch, sl st to 3rd of first 10 ch.

3rd Round: 3 ch, [3 tr(dc), 7 ch, 4 tr(dc)] into first 10ch loop, *3 tr(dc) into next 3ch sp, [4 tr(dc), 7 ch, 4 tr(dc)] into next 10ch loop, rep from * once more, 3 tr(dc) into next 3ch sp, sl st to top of first 3 ch. (Stop here for small triangle.)

4th Round: 3 ch, leaving last loop of each st on hook work 2 tr(dc) at base of 3 ch, yrh and draw through all 3 loops on hook (cluster made), *3 ch, [4 tr(dc), 5 ch, 4 tr(dc)] into next 7ch loop, 3 ch, miss next 2 tr(dc), leaving last loops of each st on hook work 3 tr(dc) into next tr(dc), yrh and draw through all 4 loops on hook (cluster made), 3 ch, miss next 2 tr(dc), 1 dc(sc) into next tr(dc), 3 ch, miss next 2 tr(dc), cluster into next tr(dc), rep from * twice more, omitting cluster from the end of the last rep and working a sl st into the top of first 3 ch.

Fig 61 Chain space
triangle

CLUSTER TRIANGLE

Ch 8, sl st in first ch to form a circle.

1st Row: 5 ch, leaving last loop of each st on hook work 3 tr(dc) into circle, yrh and draw through all 4 loops on hook (cluster made), 2 ch, (cluster, 5 ch, cluster) into circle, 2 ch, cluster into circle, 2 ch, 1 tr(dc) into circle, turn.

2nd Row: 5 ch, cluster into first 2ch sp, *2 ch, 3 tr into next 2ch sp, 2 ch*, (cluster, 2 ch, cluster) into next 5ch sp, rep from * to * once, cluster into sp formed by turning ch, 2 ch, 1 tr(dc) into 3rd turning ch, turn.

3rd Row: 5 ch, cluster into first 2ch sp, *2 ch, 2 tr(dc) into next 2ch sp, 1 tr(dc) into each of next 3 tr(dc), 2 tr(dc) into next 2ch sp, 2 ch*, (cluster, 2 ch, cluster) into next 2ch sp, rep from * to * once, cluster into sp formed by turning ch, 2 ch, 1 tr(dc) into 3rd turning ch, turn.

4th Row: 5 ch, cluster into 2ch sp, *2 ch, 2 tr(dc) into next 2ch sp, 1 tr(dc) into each tr(dc) of previous row, 2 tr(dc) into next 2ch sp, 2 ch*, (cluster, 2 ch, cluster) into next 2ch sp, rep from * to * once, cluster into sp formed by turning ch, 2 ch, 1 tr(dc) into 3rd turning ch, turn.

Continue in this manner until the triangle is the size required.

Fig 62 Cluster triangle

KNIT TRIANGLES OR TABS

These are easier to knit onto the ridges of garter stitch or purl fabric, but can be knitted separately and then sewn onto the knit side if you prefer.

Decide where you want your triangle to be. Make sure that the hem or lower edge of the item being decorated is pointing down, otherwise the add-on won't sit properly.

Pick up and knit 7 sts directly from the fabric. (For larger or smaller triangles adjust the number of stitches to the size required, always using an uneven number.)

Knit 1 row.

Dec 1 st each end of next row.

Rep these two rows once (3 sts rem).

Next row: sl 1, k2tog, psso.

Cut yarn and pull end through last stitch to tighten.

Fig 63 Knit triangles or tabs

There was always more in the world than men could see, walked they ever so slowly; they will see it no better for going fast.

JOHN RUSKIN

Arty Bits

While they are certainly fibre-related, the pieces in this section are not all meant as decorative options for adding directly to garments. Some of them would be too heavy or bulky and would likely interfere with fit and drape. Others will work well for pockets and collars, and all should work well for bags, hats, decorative cushions, journal covers, jewellery, wall hangings and so on.

To help eliminate excess bulk you can use woven fabric or craft felt as the base for the heavier pieces, rather than working them directly onto knitted or crocheted fabric. They can then be stitched or even glued to the background. This approach will also prevent distortion of the fabric, which can happen when a lot of surface texture is used.

For design inspiration look at fractals, contemporary embroidery, art quilts, the textures that surround you in your daily life, textile magazines such as the Australian publication *Textile Forum Magazine*, and *Fiberarts* from the US (see Reading List). And of course there is my favourite software, Gliftex (formerly known as Gliftic), which I use exclusively when my creative muse is on holiday (see Resources). I have included a few images generated by Gliftex at the end of this chapter.

Don't just think 'embroidery threads' for embroidery, although of course you can use those. Look through your yarn stash and dig out those amazingly textured yarns you bought years ago because you loved them. If you are like me, every time you go to a textile event or a market or Trades Hall, you come home with bits and pieces that you fully intend to use 'one day' but never get around to doing so. Now is your chance to dig them out and play with them! You can really let your hair down with the ideas in this section and use any materials you like in outrageous and unexpected combinations or aim for a subtler look if that is your preference.

Fig 64 Diffused threads

DIFFUSED THREADS

This technique is one that can be used directly on your knit or crocheted garment as it's light enough not to affect the way the garment drapes. Lengths of intensely coloured threads with sections of organza overlay can be hand or machine-stitched over the top to soften the colour intensity.

3D ADD-ONS

Metallic thread and wire crocheted together with beads, in a half-circle with increasing on the last row, will create a simple ruffled edge effect. However, you can vary this technique to create any shape you like. The combination of wire and thread allows you to 'sculpt' the shape to create raised areas.

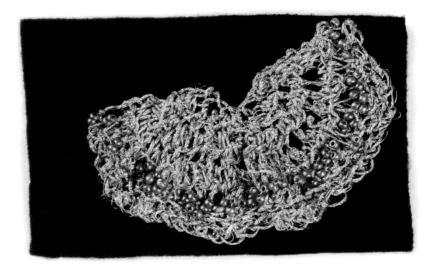

Fig 65 3D add-ons

WRAPPED PLASTIC TUBING

Interesting 'arty bits' can be made from 2 mm diameter plastic tubing wrapped in fancy thread and couched to craft felt. Plastic tubing is great for this technique in that you can bend it to your will.

Fig 66 Wrapped plastic tubing

MINIMALIST STITCHING

This is a very simple yet effective technique using small fragments of plain or patterned fabric stitched to the background. They can be applied directly to your garment fabric. To take this a step further and create a more elaborate effect you could add further embroidery stitches and beads.

Fig 67 Minimalist stitching

NEEDLEFELTING

This is a fun and easy technique with many possibilities. You can create abstract or stylised figurative images or use the technique to add areas of colour to your work. The sample in Fig 68 uses wool tops (rovings) for the outlines and silk throwster's waste in each section on crepe fabric. The sample in Fig 69 has been worked on a crocheted background using a loosely spun commercial yarn. See the Toys of the Trade chapter for more information on this technique.

Fig 68 Needlefelting with wool tops and silk throwster's waste

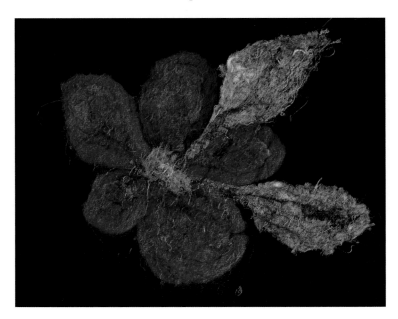

Fig 69 Needlefelting with a loosely spun commercial yarn

COUCHED STRIPS

Torn strips of organza (any light and airy fabric that will rip easily is fine) can be couched down with embroidery threads to a crocheted background. The sample also includes buttonhole stitch and diagonally wrapped stitches using a chenille-type yarn.

Fig 70 Couched strips

FIBRE-WRAPPED CORES

This is another easy way of creating wavy lines, circles and so on, resulting in decorative 3D objects that will probably work best on art works, bags or jewellery rather than garments because of the solidity of the pieces.

You can use any solid core such as tubing, chenille stems, small twigs, chopsticks, ice-cream sticks, toothpicks, skewers, etc, depending on how you want to use the finished piece.

The wrapping fibre can be torn strips of fabric, plain yarns, fancy yarns, ribbons, wool tops/rovings, in fact anything you like.

Fig 71 Fibre-wrapped cores

How to wrap

To wrap your core, lay at least a 10 cm (4 in) tail of wrapping fibre along the core—from the left to the right if you are right-handed, from right to left if you are left-handed.

Start wrapping the core back over the starting tail, keeping the wraps nice and close so that the core doesn't show through. You can make bumps in the wrapping by stopping at given intervals and doing some extra wraps, or you can opt for a more uniform appearance.

When you get to the other end cut the fibre, leaving a reasonably long tail, and using a wool needle thread the end down under the wrapping and back up again to secure.

If the end of the core is showing you can trim it close up to the fibre by pushing the wrap aside just a little and cutting the core. In the case of chenille stems you can wrap to the end, bend the end of the wrapped core over and wrap again to conceal the bend.

Attach the wrapped core to the project by couching down with a contrast or matching thread.

Knots and beads

Fig 72 Torn strips of Shibori dyed silk, randomly knotted and couched down to garter stitch fabric with beads. Beads were stitched on singly or in pairs or couched down in short lengths.

WIRE AND CHAINS

Fig 73 Wire and chains: a diagonally knitted garter stitch square with knitted 32 gauge copper wire appliqué. Crocheted chains in fancy metallic yarns have been stitched down in a random pattern using a running stitch between the chain stitches.

PAPER, FELT AND BEADS

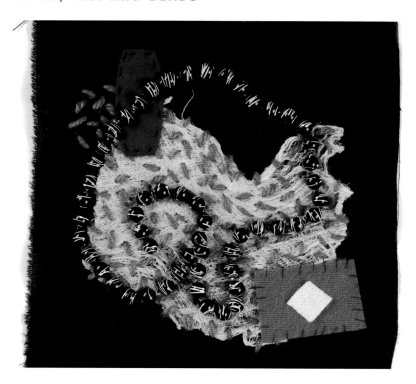

Fig 74 This piece uses paper hand-made from the inner bark of the mulberry tree (see Resources), which was dipped in cold tea before being stitched to the fabric background. Pieces of felt and beads from an old necklace were then added.

SATIN STITCH RIDGES

For this technique you use a stitch very much like satin stitch except that it is worked over a temporary core.

The height you want the ridges to be will dictate the size of inner core needed to create the effect. Be aware, however, that very high ridges may not work so well and could collapse once the core is removed. You can use string, a chunky yarn, plastic tubing, anything that won't pull apart easily. If you want your ridge to 'meander' it's best to use a core that is easily manipulated rather than the plastic tubing.

For the sample in Fig 75 I used a cord approximately 5 mm ($\frac{1}{10}$ in) in diameter.

Fig 75 Satin stitch ridges

You will need a length of inner core about 5 cm (2½ in) longer than the ridge you want to create.

Attach the satin stitch thread to the back of the background fabric where you want the ridge to start. Lay the core on the background fabric and bring the thread up to the front, close to one side of the core and taking care not to catch it.

Take the thread over to the other side of the core, back down through the fabric and then back up close to where the first stitch started.

Continue working satin stitch over the core, either in straight lines or gentle curves, until it is covered for the distance required.

Gently pull on the core to remove it from the ridge—if you have inadvertently caught the core with your thread you could cut it as close as you can to either end of the ridge and leave it inside, otherwise you will have to undo the embroidery up to where the problem is and start over from that point.

Experiment with different threads and yarns to achieve different looks.

FREEFORM STITCHING

The sample in Fig 76 shows a variety of embroidery techniques that have been used in a freeform manner. They include couching, chain stitch and cross stitch. It's a piece I'm still working on and at this point in its development I'm not sure if any other stitches will be used or if I'll stay with these three. Because of the variety of yarn textures I've used, the work looks a lot more complex than it really is, which demonstrates how a very simple approach can result in a richly textured surface.

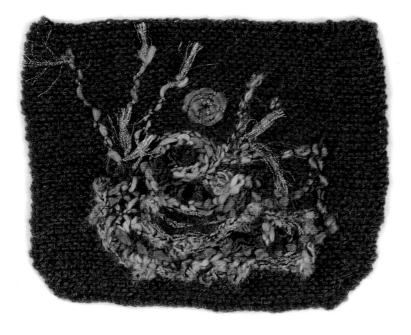

Fig 76 Freeform stitching

Congratulate yourselves if you have done something strange and extravagant and broken the monotony of a decorous age.

RALPH WALDO EMERSON

Gliftex Images for Design Inspiration

As you can see, the Gliftex software can produce some really interesting imagery with loads of potential for the adventurous, or for kick-starting a sleepy creative muse.

Fig 77a inspired the needlefelted and chain-stitched piece, 'Gold Rays'.

These images speak to me of stitching, layering, collage and beading and one day perhaps I'll have time to explore the possibilities they offer.

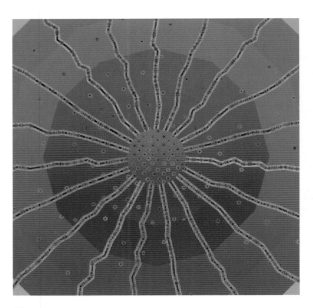

Fig 77a

Fig 77b Gold Rays

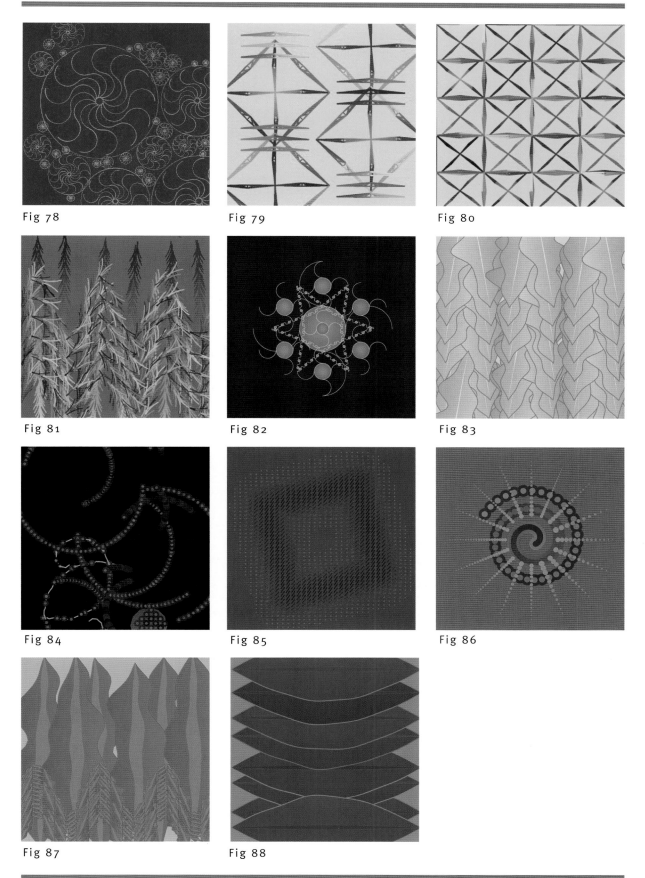

Fig 78

Fig 79

Fig 80

Fig 81

Fig 82

Fig 83

Fig 84

Fig 85

Fig 86

Fig 87

Fig 88

Changing
the Character

I begin with an idea and then it becomes something else.

PABLO PICASSO

Fig 88a

Fig 88b

I touched briefly on this technique in my second book, *FREEformations: Design and Projects in Knitting and Crochet*, and thought it would be a useful technique to expand on here. Basically, the idea is to use a much chunkier yarn and bigger needles to create a somewhat different-looking fabric to the original. This can also be done using a much finer yarn than a pattern calls for, with much bigger needles.

Figs 88a and 88b show scarves made with the same stitch pattern used in Freda's shawl (see page 133), but with different sized needles and yarns.

Not all the techniques that I investigated for the 'chunky' look were suitable, in that too many stitches were required for a pattern repeat—although this wouldn't be a problem if you wanted to knit or crochet a rug or throw, or even a coat.

If you stick to stitch patterns that require a small multiple of stitches per repeat, say no more than 8 plus edge sts, then this technique should work quite well for a scarf made with large needles or hook. If the stitch pattern calls for an even or uneven number of stitches, then you are only limited by how wide you decide the project should be. For example, the In and Out scarf (see page 106) uses just 12 sts in total because the pattern only requires an even number, making it easier to keep the scarf to a reasonable width.

Another way to use this technique and keep the width under control would be to use just one pattern repeat of a stitch pattern bordered by a plain fabric, seed (moss) stitch, garter stitch, stocking stitch or perhaps even rib.

Experiment with some of the insert patterns from the Edgings and Inserts chapter and look through your own book collection for further ideas.

Toys of the Trade

There are so many fun toys available to knitters and crocheters these days. I decided a chapter on some of them might be fun since most of them add to the decorative possibilities. It also gave me an excuse to buy some that I didn't already have!

Of course, you don't need to go buy them yourself unless you want to, as there are plenty of other ideas in the book to work with. Just in case, however, I have listed where the ones I've included can be purchased in the Resources section.

Cord-makers

Making I-cords is really easy and very fast if you have a knitting machine, and while you can easily knit a cord using double-pointed needles it is rather a slow process (see How To chapter). In between those two options are the Wonder Knitter by Clover, the Embellish-Knit (formerly the Magi-Cord) from Bond-America, and of course the more traditional knitting nancy which most of us remember from our childhood.

WONDER KNITTER

The Wonder Knitter works like a regular knitting loom except that it has a crank-handle operated by your thumb that feeds the yarn to the next peg—so all you have to do is lift each subsequent loop over the working yarn. With a regular loom you have to physically wrap each peg before lifting the previous loops, which lengthens the time required to make a cord.

EMBELLISH-KNIT

The Embellish-Knit is even easier to use since all you do is thread it up and then wind a handle. Very fast!

Fig 89 The Wonder Knitter

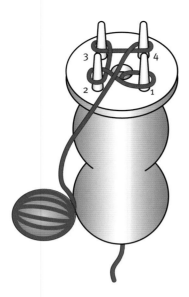

Fig 90a Traditional spool knitter (knitting nancy)

Fig 90b

Knitting nancy

The traditional cotton-reel knitting nancy can be fun, and kids love using them so I've included instructions on how to use one. You don't have to make your own these days, however, as there are various basic versions available in craft stores.

Step 1 Thread the yarn through the spool knitter from top to bottom. You may like to attach a peg to the yarn end to tension it slightly.

Step 2 Cast on by winding the yarn around the nails in an anti-clockwise direction as shown in Fig 90b. Don't pull the yarn too tightly, as this will make knitting the first round difficult.

Step 3 To knit, wind the yarn around the outside of the nails in an anti-clockwise direction.

Step 4 Using a needle or crochet hook, lift the loop on each peg up and over the yarn that has just been wound around the nails.

Continue wrapping and working in an anti-clockwise direction until the cord is the required length.

Step 5 To cast off, cut the yarn and thread it through each loop. Pull firmly to fasten off.

Hairpin fork or loom

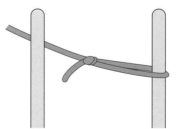

Fig. 91 Make a slip knot and place over the RH prong of the hairpin tool. Adjust so that the knot is midway between prongs.

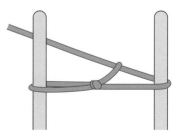

Fig. 92 Rotate the tool a half turn clockwise.

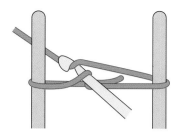

Fig. 93 Insert the hook in the slip knot.

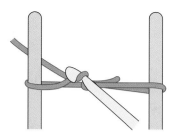

Fig. 94 Yarn round hook (yrh) and pull through.

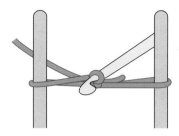

Fig. 95 Being careful not to dislodge the loop already on hook, manoeuvre the hook so that it goes backwards between both prongs and is sitting behind the RH prong.

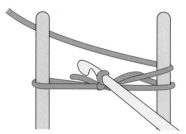

Fig. 96 Rotate the tool half a turn clockwise.

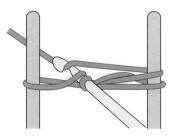

Fig. 97 Insert the hook under the front thread in the loop just made on the LH prong …

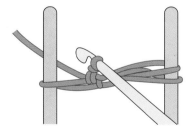

Fig. 98… and work a dc(sc).

Repeat these steps for the length required. Fasten off.

Special note: As the tool fills up, take off the bottom bar and slide off all but 5 or 6 loops. Replace the bar and roll up the strip to stop it from twisting out of shape.

LUCET

This is a great little gadget for making a square cord very easily. If you don't have a lucet but want to try the technique, you can use two pencils, a two-tined fork, a two-pronged pom-pom maker—in fact, anything with two prongs.

HOW TO USE A LUCET

Step 1 Hold the lucet in your left hand (or right hand if you are left-handed). Take the thread through the hole and hold it with your thumb. Bring yarn up and around the prongs of the lucet as shown in Fig 99a.

Step 2 Make a figure 8 around the prongs of the lucet as shown in Fig 99b. Hold the working yarn across the front of the RH prong above A.

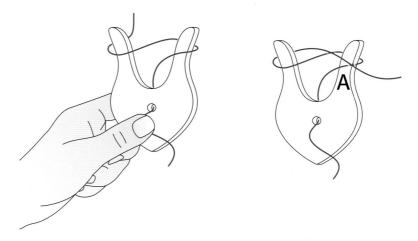

Fig 99a Step 1   Fig 99b Step 2

Step 3 With your right thumb and forefinger, lift A above the working yarn and right prong of lucet (Fig 99c). Turn the lucet clockwise so the prongs are reversed.

Step 4 Gently tighten cord as before, then take B up and over the RH prong.

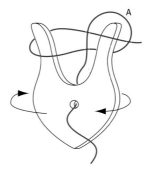
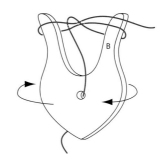

Fig 99c Step 3   Fig 99d Step 4

Step 5 Turn the lucet clockwise again and repeat steps 1 to 4 until the cord is the required length.

To finish, remove the cord from the lucet. Cut working yarn leaving a 15 cm (6 in) tail. Take the tail through the left loop and gently tighten that loop. Finally, run the tail through the right loop and pull gently to tighten.

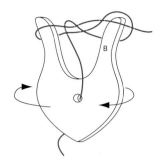

Fig 99e Step 5

Yo-Yo Maker

I had never made a Suffolk puff before discovering this little toy. They always looked way too tedious for a freeformer. Enter the Yo-Yo Maker! This tool makes short work of the process and is also foolproof if, like me, you are not so good with anything requiring precision.

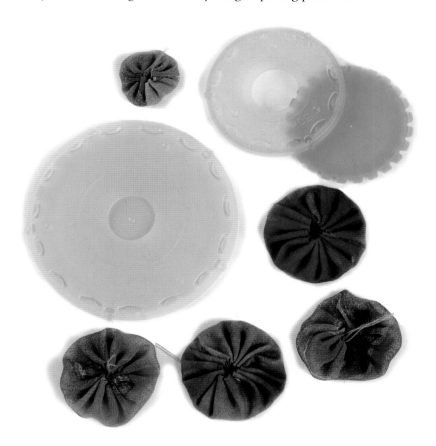

Fig 100 A Yo-Yo Maker and several samples

Pom-pom makers

Once upon a time we used two cardboard circles with a hole in the centre. Not any more. These days we have clever little tools to help make the process faster and a lot easier.

Fig 101a Various pom-pom makers

Fig 101b Pom-pom samples

Knitwit Loom flowers

Fig 102a Knitwit Loom

Fig 102b Flowers made on
a Knitwit Loom

NEEDLEFELTING

This is a fun, water and soap free way to make felt, or you can use the technique to decorate your knitted or crocheted fabric.

The process involves stabbing fibres with a special needle or needles (see Resources) until they interlock and adhere to the background fabric, which can be silk, knit fabric, crepe, in fact just about any kind of background can be used. I've not tried it but I expect certain hand-made papers could be needlefelted too.

You need a dense block of foam for your work surface—upholstery foam is good, and a foam hat-block works well too. In fact, you can place layers of wool tops over a foam hat-block and eventually create a 'felted hat'.

Many needlefelters use the technique to create three-dimensional pieces but it can be very effective for flat surface decoration. The needles have little barbs on the ends and are very sharp, so care and concentration are needed while using them and you should never allow a small child access to them.

The needles are also rather brittle and can break if flexed so try not to bend them while working.

PROJECTS

A WORD ABOUT OPTIONS ...

... GARMENT EDGINGS AND HEMS ...

As with all the garments in this book, how you finish yours in terms of edgings or hems is up to you. There are so many ways of finishing garments other than the traditional ones, ways which are so much more exciting and unique. I hope you will consider them when making any of the garment projects in this book. I've included a few ideas in the Edgings and Inserts chapter, but there are many, many others you could use.

With the exception of the Jade top (see page 167), which began with ribbing, I have added edgings after each garment was knitted because I was experimenting with ideas on ways to prevent the dreaded 'stocking stitch roll' and hoped to discover something other than the usual rib or moss stitch solution. I'm sure there is one out there but I ran out of time and had to make a decision one way or another. So I reverted to the tried and true methods mentioned above.

Please note that the patterns don't suggest needle or hook sizes for the edgings since that depends on what you choose to do.

While the use of rib and/or moss stitch certainly helps lessen the tendency of stocking stitch to roll, I also had to resort to damp ironing the edges to make them sit completely flat. To damp iron I use a damp cloth placed over the offending area and gently pressed. You can also use the traditional steaming method of holding your iron just above the fabric but I find the damp ironing method works best. You can only do this if you have used pure wool to make the garment though, since anything with acrylic in it will not bounce back. If you have used an acrylic or wool blend, I would use the light steam method—holding the iron just above the fabric and pressing the 'shot of steam' button.

... DECORATING OPTIONS

There are so many decorative options out there that could be used on garments and accessories and this book only covers a handful of what I wanted to include, with many more left out due to time and space restrictions. Enjoy the ones you find in *Surface Works* but do continue to explore, experiment and discover.

TIP: If you add the edging after sewing the garment together you will find it easier to use circular needles because of the number of stitches required.

A Collection of Bags

Almost Autumn

I've not done a lot of felting, so if you have please feel free to felt the strips the way you would normally do it.

Fig 103

YOU WILL NEED

200 g (7 oz) Cleckheaton 'Country' 8-ply

small amount of wool rovings (a few grams [ounces] is plenty) in colours to suit your project

3 x 2.5 cm (1 in) rubber O-rings or plastic curtain rings

16 assorted beads to complement wool colours

one 2 cm (¾ in) button

size 4 mm (F/5) crochet hook

size 3 mm (D/3) crochet hook

INSTRUCTIONS

BAG PANELS
Make 2.

Using 4 mm (F/5) hook, ch 39.

1st Row: 1 htr(hdc) in 3rd ch from hook, htr(hdc) to end, 1 ch, turn.

2nd Row: 1 htr(hdc) in first st, htr(hdc) to end, 1 ch, turn.

Rep 2nd row until work measures 25 cm (10 in). 1 ch, turn and work 'shell' edging as follows:

1 dc in first st, miss 1 st, in next stitch work *1 dc(sc), 1 htr(hdc), 1 tr(dc), 1 htr(hdc), 1 dc(sc) (shell made), miss 1 st, 1 dc(sc) in next st, miss 1 st, rep from * to last 2 sts, miss 1 st, dc(sc) in last st. Fasten off.

FELTED STRIPS
Separate a 2 cm x 1 m (½ x 40 in) strip from the rovings.

Place some hand-hot water in the kitchen sink or a large basin with a little detergent. Drop the strip into the bowl and wet thoroughly, working in the detergent so it's nice and soapy.

Rub vigorously between your hands, up and down the length of fibre, until it has felted, adding extra hot water during the process as required. If you like you can rub the strip between two pieces of bubble wrap, bubble sides together, to aid the process. The strip is felted when you can no longer separate the fibres by pulling them apart.

Rinse, squeeze out excess water and set aside to dry.

You need to felt enough fibre to make 32 x 10 cm (4 in) strips and 3 x 25 cm (10 in) strips.

Sew a line of tacking stitches strips across the width of the bag about 9 cm (3½ in) from the top of the shell edging; this marks the location of the felted strips.

Centre the short strips along this line, making sure to stagger them slightly, and pin into place.

Sew the strips in place by working a row of running stitch, making sure to catch each strip as you stitch. The stitching won't be seen so you can double back at any time to make sure each strip is secure.

Leaving a little overhanging at each side, lay the long strips across the centre of the short strips and stitch down at each end and in the centre. Take the overlap to the wrong side of the bag and stitch down to secure.

RINGS

Work dc(sc) around the rings until covered, then work 2 dc(sc) in each stich around inner circle. Sew the rings into position as shown in the project sample.

FINISHING

With wrong sides together and starting just below the shell edging at the top left-hand corner, join bag panels by working dc(sc) through both thicknesses around all sides of the panels.

Make chain loop by joining yarn to the dc(sc) on the RH side of 5th shell on back panel, ch 12, sl st to dc(sc) on LH side of centre shell, turn and work sl st back along chain, ending with a sl st in first dc(sc)

Sew button to top of bag in front of the centre shell

BEAD DANGLES

Using 3 mm (D/3) hook, make 25 ch. Fasten off leaving a 20 cm (8 in) tail. Thread 5 beads onto tail knot end securely and trim. Make 2.

Make another chain length of 20 ch, fasten off leaving a 20 cm (8 in) tail. Thread 3 beads onto tail, knot and trim. Make 2.

Sew one short and one long bead dangle to either side of bag just above the horizontal felted strips.

STRAP

Using 3 mm (D/3) hook, ch 4, work 1 dc(sc) into 2nd ch from hook, dc(sc) to end. Work 2 more rows.

4th Row: Inc 1 st at each end of row.

5th Row: 1 ch, dc(sc)in 2nd st from hook, dc(sc) to end.

Rep 5th row until strap measures 96 cm (38 in). Fasten off.

Sew strap to each inside corner of bag.

Fig 104

YOU WILL NEED

50 g (1¾ oz) La Lana Wools 'Wool Worsted' (Col A)

50 g (1¾ oz) Plymouth Yarns 'Encore Colorspun' (Col B)

assortment of beads in various sizes and colours to suit:

> 4 x 1.5 cm (½ in) beads
>
> 4 x ½ cm (¼ in) beads
>
> 15 x size 6 bead
>
> 9 x size 11 bead
>
> 3 clear glass seed beads

5.5 mm (US9) needles

4.5 mm (US7) needles

4 mm crochet hook

beading thread

wool needle for sewing up and a finer needle for attaching the beads

Gauge is not critical for this project.

INSTRUCTIONS

Stitch pattern

1st Row: With Col A, k to end.

2nd Row: With Col A, p to end.

****3rd Row:** With Col B, k1, *yfw, sl 1 p-wise, ybk, k1, rep from * to last st, k1.

4th Row: With Col B, p to end.

5th Row: With Col A, k2, *yfwd, sl 1 p-wise, ybk, k1, rep from * to end.

6th Row: As 2nd row.

FRONT PANEL

With Col A and larger needles, cast on 36 sts and knit 6 rows of pattern as described above.

Rep rows 3 to 6 until work measures 15 cm (6 in). Fasten off Col B.

Change to smaller needles and work in st st for 11 rows.

Next row: purl.

Make a row of eyelets as follows: k1, *k2tog, fwd, rep from * to last st, k1.

Work 5 rows 1 x 1 rib. Cast off.**

BACK PANEL
Pick up and knit 36 sts from cast-on edge of front panel, purl 1 row.

Rep instructions as for front panel from ** to **.

FINISHING
Sew sides of bag together using mattress stitch (see How To chapter).

Along bottom edge of bag, using smaller needles with Col B, pick up and knit 8 sts.

*Dec one st at both ends of next and every alternate row until 2 sts rem, k2tog, cast off leaving a 6 cm (2½ in) tail.

Make 3 more triangles in the same manner.

Thread 2 beads onto each tail, tie a knot to secure and trim end.

Thread 8 smaller beads onto beading thread plus one of the clear glass seed beads to act as a turning bead. Miss this last bead, take thread back up through all the other beads and secure to bag between two of the triangles. Repeat between all triangles.

STRAP
I made the strap for this project using a lucet (see Toys of the Trade chapter). If you don't have a lucet you can make an I-cord instead (see How To chapter).

Using Col B, make a cord approx 65 cm (26 in) long.

Sew strap to the side seams inside the rib section of the bag.

DRAWSTRING CORD
With Col A make 90 ch, fasten off. Thread a length of Col B through the chain stitches for the length of the cord. Tie yarns together and thread back through cord.

Thread cord through eyelet holes and, finally, tie a knot at each end.

Monet

YOU WILL NEED

150 g (5½ oz) Cleckheaton 'Country' 8-ply (Col A)

1 ball Plymouth Yarns 'Rimini Rainbow' (Col B)

1 ball Plymouth Yarns 'Ms Jones' (Col C); you won't use much so there'll be plenty left over for another project!

Fig 105a Front of bag

4.5 mm (7) needles

wool needle

30 cm (12 in) length of cord, approximately 5 mm (0.2 in) in diameter

for the handles:

52 x 12 mm (½ in) wooden beads

24 x 8 mm (0.3 in) green glass beads

2 x 40 cm (16 in) 16-gauge craft wire (or 20-gauge wire doubled, then twisted together)

(see How To chapter for instructions on making the handles)

Finished size of bag is approximately 23 x 24 cm (9 x 9½ in).

Exact gauge is not critical.

Fig 105b Back of bag

INSTRUCTIONS

BAG PANEL
Make 2.

Special instructions
M1—k into loop between the st just worked and the next st on the LH needle. Do this by inserting left needle under the yarn between the stitches on each needle, from back to front, and then k that stitch by working into the front loop on the needle, twisting the strand of yarn.
PM—place marker.

Stitch pattern (multiple of 8 sts +1).

1st Row: (WS) p1, *k1, p1, k5, p1, rep from * to end.

2nd Row: k1, *p5, k1, p1, k1, rep from * to end.

3rd Row: p1, *M1, (k1, p1, k1 all into next st), M1, p1, p5tog, p1, rep from * to end.

4th, 6th and 8th Rows: k1, *p1, k1, p5, k1, rep from * to end of row.

5th and 7th Rows: p1, *k5, p1, k1, p1, rep from * to end of row.

9th Row: p1, *p5tog, p1, M1, (k1, p1, k1 all into next st), M1, p1, rep from * to end of row.

10th Row: Repeat 2nd row.

11th Row: Repeat 1st row.

12th Row: Repeat 2nd row.

Using size 5 mm (US8) needles, cast on 64 sts. Starting on WS row, work 25 sts in stitch pattern, place marker (PM), k14, PM, and work 25 sts in pattern to end of row. Turn, and work 25 sts in row 2 of pattern, PM, p14, PM, and work remaining 25 sts in stitch pattern.

Continue as established, working centre 14 sts in reverse st st (p on RS, k on WS) and first and last 25 sts in stitch pattern for a total of 6 reps of the stitch pattern (72 rows). Cast off.

HANDLE CARRIER

Cast off 16 sts, p to end of row.

Next row: Cast off 16 sts, then work in 4 x 4 rib over remaining 32 sts for 16 rows. Cast off.

DECORATING THE BAG

Weave lengths of Col B through the knit stitch channels either side of the bumps, as indicated in the photographs.

For the centre panel, lay the cord down as indicated in the sample, and with Col C, work a satin stitch ridge (see page 70) over the top of it for its entire length, letting the cord meander.

For the random flowers, take short lengths of Col B and work two or three satin stitches as shown in the photographs.

FINISHING

Sew sides of bag together using mattress stitch (see How To chapter).

Fold rib section over handle and stitch down to inside of bag.

Stitch ends of handle carrier together, using mattress stitch to ensure that the join in the beaded handle doesn't move from inside the carrier.

VARIATION

You can opt to leave the reverse side of the bag plain or to decorate it using a completely different technique.

Lavender Mist

Fig 106

YOU WILL NEED

100 g (3½ oz) Cleckheaton 'Country Silk' 8-ply (Col A)

50 g ball Plymouth Yarns 'Tomorrow' (Col B)

4.5 mm (G/6) hook

4 mm (F/5) hook

2 cm (½ in) button for closure

2 large and 2 small square paillettes (from Trendsetter Yarns)

Gauge is not critical for this project

Finished size is approximately 19 cm (7½ in) in diameter.

INSTRUCTIONS

CIRCLE
Make 2.

1st Round: With Col A, wind yarn twice around forefinger one and a half times, make 1 ch over the yarn to secure circle and to count as first dc(sc). Work a further 7 dc(sc) into circle, join with sl st to first dc(sc) (8 dc[sc]).

Pull loose end of yarn to tighten circle.

2nd Round: With Col A, work 1 ch then 1 dc(sc) in st at base of ch, 2 dc(sc) in each st around circle, join with sl st to first ch (16 sts).

3rd Round: With Col B, 1 ch to count as first st, 1 dc(sc) into base of ch, [1 dc(sc) into next dc(sc), 2 dc(sc) into next dc(sc)] 7 times, 1 dc(sc) into last dc(sc). Join with sl st to first ch (24 sts).

4th Round: With Col A, 1 ch, 1 dc(sc) into st at base of ch, [1 dc(sc) into each of next 2 dc(sc), 2 dc(sc) into next dc(sc)] 7 times, 1 dc(sc) into each of next 2 dc(sc), join with sl st to first ch (32 sts).

Continue working in rounds, alternating yarns and increasing as follows:

5th Round: Inc in every 4th st (40 sts).

6th Round: Work without increasing (40 sts).

7th Round: Inc in every 5th st (48 sts).

8th Round: Inc in every 6th st (56 sts).

9th Round: Inc in every 7th st (64 sts).

10th Round: Inc in every 8th st (72 sts).

11th Round: Inc in every 9th st (80 sts).

12th Round: Inc in every 10th st (88 sts).

13th Round: Inc in every 11th st (96 sts).

14th Round: Work without increasing.

Fasten off, leaving a small tail as a marker. Count 24 sts from finishing position and place marker in 24th stitch.

Repeat for second circle.

GUSSET AND STRAP
Col A 'Country Silk'

Col B 'Tomorrow'

Note: To avoid too many yarn ends you will be working two rows with Col A and then carrying it back under the stitches of the Col B row to the other side of the work.

1st Row: With 4 mm (F/5) hook and Col A, make 7 ch, miss first ch, dc(sc) in each ch to end, 1 ch, turn.

2nd Row: With Col A, 1 dc(sc) in each st to end, 1 ch, turn. Join in Col B.

3rd Row: With Col B and working over Col A, work 1 dc(sc) in each st to end, drop Col B, 1 ch, turn.

4th Row: With Col A work 2 rows dc(sc), drop Col A.

Rep rows 3 and 4 until strap measures 120 cm (47 in).

Join ends of strap.

FINISHING
Making sure the join of the strap is at the bottom of the bag, hold wrong sides together and using dc(sc), join one circle to the strap, using back loop only of the stitches at the circle edges.

Repeat for other circle.

Join Col A to centre of opening (should be at the 12th st) and with 4 mm (F/5) hook make a chain loop to fit around your chosen closure. Attach other end of loop to the 13th st. Fasten off and sew in all ends.

Sew button to front of bag.

Sew square paillettes to front of bag as shown in the photograph.

Ruffles

YOU WILL NEED

120 g (4¼ oz) Cleckheaton 'Country' 8-ply #2271 (Col A)

small amounts of the following:

     Plymouth Yarns 'Hot Hot Hot' #681 (Col B)

     Cleckheaton 'Country Naturals' #1832 (Col C)

     Plymouth Yarns 'Jungle' #5 (Col D)

4.5 mm (US7) needles

3.75 mm (US5) needles

wool needle

pair of acrylic handles

Fig 107

INSTRUCTIONS

BAG PANELS
Make 2.

With Col A and larger needles, cast on 46 sts.

Knit 3 rows in st st.

4th Row: (WS) with Col B knit one row of fluffle st (see Textured Stitches chapter).

5th to 9th Rows: Starting with knit row, work 5 rows of st st.

10th Row: Using Col C, purl.

11th to 15th Rows: Using Col C, knit.

16th Row: Using Col D, knit.

17th to 25th Rows: Using Col A, work in st st.

26th Row: (WS) With Col A, purl 14 st, knit fluffle st for 20 sts, p14.

27th Row: Knit.

Rep last two rows 9 times.

46th Row: Using Col A, purl.

Rows 47 to 52: Using Col A, work in st st.

Rows 53 to 57: Using Col C, knit. Break off Col C.

58th Row: (WS) Join in Col D and knit one row.

Using Col A, knit 3 rows st st.

62nd Row: (WS) Using Col D, knit one row.

Using Col A, knit 2 rows st st.

HANDLE CARRIER
65th Row: Cast off 8 sts, knit to end.

66th Row: Cast off 8 sts, purl to end.

Change to smaller needles and knit 20 rows of 4 x 4 rib over remaining stitches. Cast off.

Fold rib section over handle and stitch down. Repeat for other side.

Putting on the Glitz

Although this book is about surface decoration, not all fabrics need it. There will be times when pure and simple is the look you want, or when the yarn you use needs no other adornment. Such is the case with Sari Silk, a beautiful fibre with its own unique texture. However, I wanted to add just a little bit of Eastern exotic bling to this bag so I used a very fine strand of Lurex with the main yarn.

Fig 108

YOU WILL NEED

200 g (7 oz) Himalaya Yarn 'Sari Silk'

small amount of fine gold Lurex (available on cones from machine-knitting yarn suppliers)

one 5.5 mm (US9) and one 6.5 mm (US10.5) knitting needle (you can use same size needles if you like)

5 mm (US8) needles

4 mm (F/5) crochet hook

1 chenille stem (available from craft stores)

3 accent beads and 1 seed bead, beading thread and needle to fit through beads

wool needle

INSTRUCTIONS

BAG PANELS
Make 2.

Purl side of fabric is right side.

With one end of Sari Silk and one end of Lurex, using the larger needles, cast on 40 sts and knit in st st until work measures 16 cm (6¼ in).

Change to 5 mm (US8) needles and continue in 1 x 1 rib until rib section measures 10 cm (4 in). Cast off.

With wrong sides together and starting 4 cm (1½ in) from top, join sides and lower edge of bag together with one row of dc(sc), ending 4 cm (1½ in) below top of bag.

Sew the remaining 4 cm (1½ in) of rib sections so that the seam is on the inside.

At the centre front and back, fold centre of rib section over until it sits at the junction where the reverse stocking stitch and rib meet and pin into place. This forms a gentle curve with the sides of the bag sitting higher. Stitch hem down.

Turn bag so bottom edge is at the top and work triangles as follows:

SMALL SIDE TRIANGLE
Using Sari Silk only, pick up and knit 7 sts in from side edge.

1st Row: Knit.

2nd Row: k2tog, k3, k2tog.

3rd Row: Knit.

4th Row: k2tog, k1, k2tog.

5th Row: sl 1, k2tog, psso, fasten off.

Large centre triangle

Using Sari Silk, pick up and knit 13 sts from alongside first triangle.

1st Row: Knit.

2nd Row: k2tog, k9, k2tog.

3rd Row: Knit.

4th Row: k2tog, k7, k2tog.

5th Row: Knit.

6th Row: k2tog, k5, k2tog.

Continue decreasing as established until 3sts remain.

Next Row: sl 1, k2tog, psso, fasten off.

Repeat small triangle for other side.

Strap

With 4 mm hook, make 4 ch using Sari Silk.

1st Row: 1 dc(sc) in 2nd ch from hook, dc(sc) to end, 1 ch, turn.

2nd Row: 1 dc(sc) in each st to end, 1 ch, turn.

Rep 2nd row until strap measures 76 cm (30 in). Fasten off. Sew to inside seams of bag.

Closure

Using Sari Silk, work a row of dc(sc) over chenille stem, bending it into a circle measuring about 8 cm (3 in) in diameter. Wrap the ends of the stem around each other to join and work a few extra dc(sc) over the join. Sew circle to centre of folded hem.

Thread beads, with the seed bead threaded last.

Take thread back up through all but the seed bead. Fasten off securely.

Using Sari Silk, make a chain length about 130 cm (52 in) long, fold it and with a large safety pin attached to folded end, thread the cord through the hem section of the bag. Draw up until bag opening is about 13 cm (5 in) wide and tie a loose knot to secure.

Aztec

YOU WILL NEED

100 g (3½ oz) Cleckheaton 'Country' 8-ply

small amounts of fancy yarns for embroidery (I used Plymouth Yarns 'Noch Eros', 'Patches', 'Jungle' and 'Parrot', left over from the Spiral cushion, page 123)

size 4.5 mm (US7) knitting needles

size 3.5 mm (E/4) crochet hook

pair of rattan eye-shaped bag handles

wool needle

Fig 109

Special instruction

This bag is worked using short rows (SR). Please refer to How To chapter
if you are unfamiliar with this technique.

Instructions

Bag panels

Make 2.

Cast on 40 sts.

*Knit 35, work SR, purl back along row.

Knit 30, work SR, purl back along row.

Knit 25, work SR, purl back along row.

Knit 20, work SR, purl back along row.

Knit 15, work SR, purl back along row.

Knit 10, work SR, purl back along row.

Knit 5, work SR, purl back along row*.

Knit 10 rows stocking stitch across all sts.

Rep SR sequence as before from * to *.

Knit 1 row across all stitches.

**Purl 35, work SR, knit back along row.

Purl 30, work SR, knit back along row.

Purl 25, work SR, knit back along row.

Purl 20, work SR, knit back along row.

Purl 15, work SR, knit back along row.

Purl 10, work SR, knit back along row.

Purl 5, work SR, knit back along row**.

Knit 6 rows st st across all stitches.

Rep SR sequence from ** to **.

Purl 1 row across all stitches.

Rep SR sequence 1 from * to *.

Knit 1 row across all stitches, cast off loosely.

Embroidered panel

Since the embroidery is to be worked randomly and in a freeform manner, it's not possible to give detailed instructions. Instead I have listed some suggestions to get you started. You can use similar yarns to the ones I've listed above, or raid your own stash for suitable yarns, keeping in mind that you will need at least three different textures.

Firstly you need to mark off the V-shaped section for the embroidered area. To do this, run a row of tacking stitches along the short row shaping line on either side of centre.

Fill in this area with densely worked embroidery using the following ideas:

- chain lengths made with the fancy yarns which are then attached with a short running stitch
- randomly placed chain or straight stitches
- French knots
- satin stitch
- lengths of fancy yarns couched down with contrasting threads.

Keep working until the entire area has been filled with embroidery.

Add beads in amongst the embroidery if you like to add further richness to the surface.

Add bead dangles to plain sections of front panel if required.

Handle carrier

With main yarn and 4.5 mm (7) needles, pick up and knit 32 sts across narrow edge of bag. Starting with a purl row knit 15 rows stocking stitch. Cast off.

Lower edging

Following the pattern below, knit the edging until it 'fits' the bottom edge of the bag as shown in the photograph (5 pattern repeats should do it).

Cast on 6 sts.

1st, 2nd and 3rd Rows: Knit.

4th Row: Cast on 3 sts, k to end.

5th, 6th and 7th Rows: Knit.

8th Row: Cast on 3 sts, k to end.

9th, 11th, 13th, 14th and 15th Rows: Knit.

10th and 12 Rows: Purl.

16th Row: Cast off 3 sts, k to end.

17th, 18th and 19th Rows: Knit.

20th Row: Cast off 3 sts, k to end.

These 20 rows form the pattern.

Finishing

With wrong sides of bag panels together, sandwich the edging between the panels and crochet a row of surface chain stitch (see How To chapter) through all three pieces, making sure to work on the very edge of each piece to avoid a bulky seam. You may find it easier to tack the edging to the back panel first.

Join the panels together with a row of dc(sc).

Fold handle carrier over handle and stitch down to inside of bag.

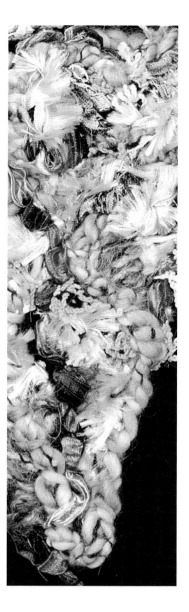

Scarves and Hats

The In and Out scarf

Fig 110

YOU WILL NEED

170 g (6 oz) Cleckheaton 'Gusto' # 10

15 mm (US19) needles

optional: Pom-Pom Maker

CROSS STITCH PATTERN

1st Row: *insert needle behind first stitch and knit into the back of the 2nd stitch, then knit the first stitch, and slip both sts off the needle together. Rep from * to end.

2nd Row: p1, *p 2nd stitch, then the first stitch and slip both sts off the needle together, rep from * to last st, p 1.

INSTRUCTIONS

Cast on 12 sts.

1st Row: Purl.

Knit 8 rows of pattern.

Knit 6 rows of st st.

Knit 8 rows of pattern.

Continue knitting 6 rows of st st and 8 rows of pattern until scarf measures 138 cm (54 in) or length required, ending with 8 rows of pattern. Cast off.

You may like to pin and steam the stocking stitch sections to prevent them from rolling in quite so much.

VARIATIONS

Use garter stitch instead of stocking stitch for the plain sections.

Add three pom-poms as shown in the photograph, or decorate as you wish.

Purple Haze

Fig 111

YOU WILL NEED

100 g (3½ oz) Sirdar 'Evita' or yarn of your choice with similar gauge

small amount of silk curls or wool tops/roving for needlefelting

9 mm (US13) needles

needlefelting needle (see Resources)

dense foam block (see Resources)

INSTRUCTIONS

1st Row: Cast on one stitch. Knit into front then into back of this stitch (2 sts).

2nd Row: Knit into front then into back of first stitch (3 sts).

Continue working in garter stitch, increasing at the beginning of each row until 20 sts or width required for scarf.

Change to 2 x 2 rib and knit until scarf rib section measures 94 cm (36 in) or length required.

Using garter stitch, decrease at the beginning of each row until 1 st remains.

NEEDLEFELTING EMBELLISHMENT

If you are new to needlefelting, refer to the basic instructions in the Toys of the Trade chapter before continuing.

Note: It is very important that you keep your fingers out of the way of the felting needle to avoid injury.

Lay scarf over the foam block surface, spreading it slightly so you can easily see the channels created by the purl stitches.

Work along these channels, gradually building up a narrow layer of colour by adding pieces of the silk curls and prodding them into the base fabric with the needle until they adhere to the surface.

Add a tassel at each end if desired.

Fluffle

Fig 112

Refer to instructions for fluffle stitch in the Textured Stitches chapter.

YOU WILL NEED

100 g (3½ oz) 8-ply (DK), 25 g (1 oz) of a chenille type yarn or similar, and
1 ball of Trendsetter's 'Checkmate' yarn or similar. This yarn needs
to have holes or gaps for the hook to be able to be inserted through
it. A very soft ribbon will also work.

5 mm (USH/8) crochet hook

Gauge is not critical for this project.

INSTRUCTIONS

Make 200 ch.

1st Row: 1 tr(dc) in 6th ch from hook, *1 ch, miss 1 tr(dc), 1 tr(dc) in
next ch, rep from * to end, 1 ch, turn.

2nd Row: Leaving a 20 cm (8 in) tail, join in fancy yarn and work a row
of fluffle st. If using 'Checkmate' or any other yarn that has solid sections
in it, when you reach a solid bit work dc(sc) with both yarns held
together. At the end of the solid section revert to fluffle st again. At the
end of this row, cut fancy yarn leaving a 20 cm (8 in) tail, work 4 ch in
plain yarn, turn.

3rd Row: Miss 1 dc(sc), work 1 tr(dc) in next st, *1 ch, miss 1 dc(sc), 1
tr(dc) in next st, rep from * to end, 1 ch, turn.

4th Row: Work a row of fluffle st, 4 ch, turn.

Rep rows 3 and 4 three more times, then 3rd row once. Fasten off both
yarns leaving a 20 cm (8 in) tail of fancy yarn only.

Join in chenille yarn, leaving the long tail, and work a row of tr(dc),
working into each 1ch sp and tr(dc) along row.

At this point you can work back along the row with another row of
tr(dc) or you can fasten off, once again leaving the long tail, join chenille
to other side of scarf and work a row of tr(dc) to match the first side.

Fill in spaces between the fancy yarn fringes with some chenille fringes.

Basic Crocheted Hat

YOU WILL NEED

100 g (3½ oz) La Lana Wools 'Knitting Worsted' or an 8-ply yarn that will felt

5 mm (H/8) crochet hook

coloured felt: I used felt sheets from La Lana Wools but you could use craft felt (although it's acrylic and not as thick)

10–12 size 8 seed beads in colours to suit project

Finished measurement

Fits 53–56 cm (21–23 in) head.

Fig 113a

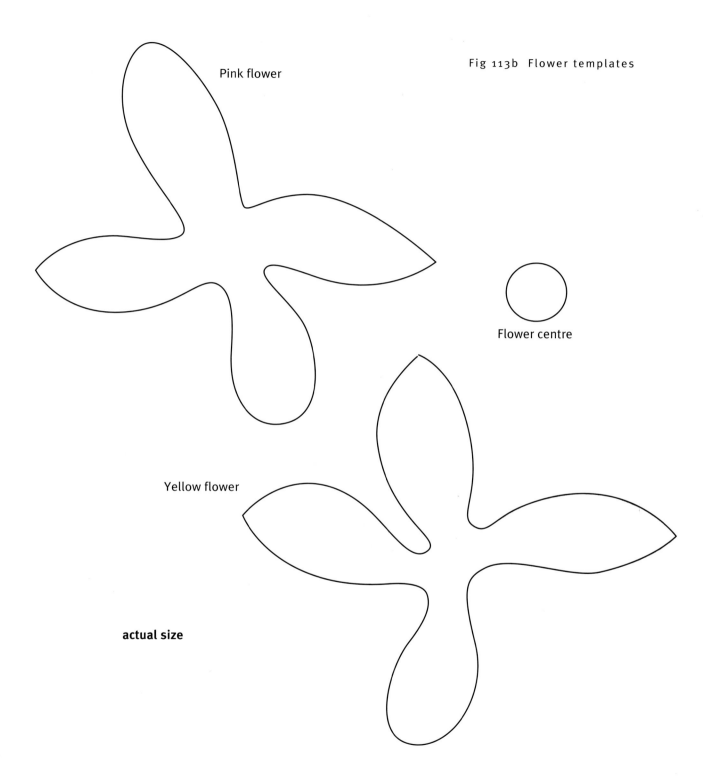

Pink flower

Fig 113b Flower templates

Flower centre

Yellow flower

actual size

INSTRUCTIONS

Make 4 ch and join into with a sl st into a circle.

1st Round: 8 dc(sc) into circle.

2nd Round: 1 ch, 2 dc into each st around circle, join with sl st to first dc(sc) of previous round.

3rd Round: 1 ch, increase in every 2nd st around circle, join round.

4th Round: 1 ch, increase in every 3rd st around circle, join round.

Continue working in rounds, increasing as established for a further 4 rounds.

Change to tr(dc) and work 9 rounds without shaping.

Work one row of crab st (reverse double crochet) around edge.

Cut two felt flowers and two centres using templates provided. Sew to hat as shown in the sample.

Sew beads to flower centres.

Basic Knitted Hat

You will need

2 x 50 g (3½ oz) balls Cleckheaton 'Country' 8-ply

4.5 mm (US7) needles

5 mm (US8) needles

Gauge: 18 sts and 24 rows to 10 cm (4 in). This gauge makes a hat that is a snug fit so you might like to use a slightly bigger needle size for a looser style.

Fig 114

INSTRUCTIONS

Cast on 88 sts with 4.5 mm (US7) needles and knit 10 rows st st.

Change to 5 mm (US8) needles and knit st st until work measures 17 cm (6¾ in) from beginning.

SHAPE CROWN

1st Row: (RS) *k9 sts, k2tog, rep from * to end of row.

2nd and all alternate rows: Purl.

3rd Row: *k8, k2tog, rep from * to end of row.

5th Row: *k7, k2tog, rep from * to end of row.

7th Row: *k6, k2tog, rep from * to end of row.

Continue shaping as established, knitting one less st before each decrease until 16 sts remain.

Next Row: p2tog 8 times.

Next Row: k2tog 4 times, cut yarn leaving a long tail.

Thread tail through last 4 sts and pull to tighten.

Sew side seam using mattress stitch, reversing the seam for the final 4 cm (1½ in) of seam so that the seam is hidden on the rolled brim.

Decorate as required using any of the ideas in this book.

Sue's Hat

My friend Sue made this felted hat (decorated with La Lana 'Jewels' left over from the Walnut vest project on page 172) and has kindly allowed me to include it here. Neither she nor I is an experienced felter and, since both of us have a front-loading washing machine, Sue decided to hand-felt the hat rather than risk things going wrong in the machine. As you can see it worked out really well. In fact, Sue said the felting process was really easy so it would seem that the yarn definitely wanted to be felted! Her felting instructions follow the pattern.

Fig 115 This hat, with its crown and brim shaped differently, also appears with the Walnut vest (page 172).

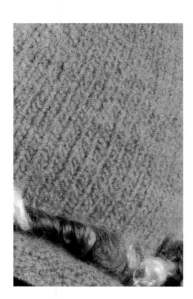

YOU WILL NEED

La Lana Wools 'Knitting Worsted':

    1 x 113 g (4 oz) hank

    or 165 (183, 215) metres

    or 180 (200, 235) yards

La Lana Wools 'Jewels' for trim: 84 cm (33 in)

7.5 mm (US11) circular needle, 40 cm (16 in) long

NOTES

- *Gauge:* approximately 3 sts to 2.5 cm (1 in).
- *Three sizes:* approximately 50 (55, 60) cm or 20 (22, 24) inches in circumference.
- *Option:* to make the rounded, smooth top seen here (instead of the cowboy style crown seen with the Walnut vest), work to approximately 18 cm (7 in) instead of 20 cm (8 in) for the crown.

Special instructions

Stocking stitch—plain knit all rounds.

M1—Insert left needle from front to back under horizontal strand between last stitch worked and next stitch on left needle, form a loop on left needle. Knit in back loop of this stitch to avoid making a hole.

INSTRUCTIONS

Cast on 80 (90, 100) sts with circular needles, place marker, join and knit 1 round, purl 1 round.

Next Round: *k8 (9,10), M1, rep from * increasing to 90 (100, 110) sts.

Purl 1 round.

Knit rounds until you have 5 cm (2 in) from cast-on edge. Then *k7 (8, 9), k2tog, rep from * (80, 90, 100 sts).

Knit 5 cm (2 in) more. Approx 12.5 cm (5 in) from cast-on round, place marker to indicate start of crown.

CROWN

1st Round: (small) *k2tog (40 sts).
(medium) *k2tog 4 times, k1, rep from * (50 sts).
(large) *k2tog 4 times, k2, rep from * (60 sts).

2nd and 3rd Rounds: knit

4th Round: (small) *k2, M1, repeat from * (60 sts).

(medium — *k2, M1, k3, M1, repeat from * (70 sts).
(large) *k3, M1, repeat from * (80 sts).

Continue working in the round until work measures approximately 18cm (7cm) or 20 cm (8 in) if you are making the style seen on page 171.

TOP SHAPING
(change to double-pointed needles when needed)

1st Round 1: k4 (5, 6), k2tog, repeat from * (50, 60, 70 sts).

2nd, 3rd, 5th, 6th, 8th, 10th and 12th Rounds: Knit.

4th Round: *k3 (4, 5), k2tog *repeat from * (40, 50, 60 sts).

7th Round: *k2 (3, 4), k2tog, rep from * (30, 40, 50 sts).

9th Round: *k1 (2, 3), k2tog, rept from * (20, 30, 40 sts).

11th Round: *k0 (1, 2), k2tog, rep from * (10, 20, 30 sts).

13th Round: k2tog around (5, 10, 15 sts).

14th Round: (medium and large only) k2tog around (5, 8 sts).

15th Round: (large only) k2tog around (4 sts).

Cut yarn and with tapestry needle thread through remaining sts. Fasten off. Secure all other yarn ends

HAND-FELTING
Note: If you are conversant with the felting process using a washing machine and prefer to felt the hat in that way, ignore these instructions.

You will need a bowl of similar size to your head, or a hat form if you have one; Sunlight soap flakes, and rubber gloves.

Throw hat into laundry tub with very hot water and lots of soap and knead vigorously until the felting process starts.

Continue kneading but keep checking size, stopping when the hat fits the bowl or hat form.

When required size is reached, rinse hat well until all traces of the soap are gone. Place on the bowl or hat form to dry. It will take about three days to dry completely.

DECORATION
Wrap the trim around the base of the crown and tie a knot. You can stitch the trim to the hat if you like but I chose not to so I could change the trim if I wanted to.

All about Cushions

We all love cushions to relax against or to sit on or to use as support, and because they are used this way they need to be practical and easily cleaned. Decorative cushions, on the other hand, are usually reserved for bedrooms or formal lounge/sitting rooms—or completely non-existent if kids and pets abound. My lounge chair has a heap of cushions that are sat on, leant on, tossed on the floor, etcetera, but none are appreciated simply for their magnificence! I thought it might be fun to create some designs that 'please the eye' rather than just being useful!

Blue Radial

Fig 116

YOU WILL NEED

100 g (3½ oz) ball Cleckheaton 'Country Mohair'

1 ball Moda Vera 'Lasagna' (this is a flat felt-like yarn and if you are unable to find the one I've used, you could substitute 12 mm (½ in) wide strips of felt or a ribbon yarn

1 ball Plymouth Yarns 'Odyssey Glitz'

5.5 mm (US9) knitting needles

5 mm (USH) crochet hook

36 cm (14 in) round cushion blank

wool needle

INSTRUCTIONS

This cushion is worked using short rows (SR). If you are unfamiliar with the technique it may be helpful to practise it first following the instructions in the How To chapter.

Cast on 34 sts.

Knit 2 rows.

3rd Row: Knit 30, work SR, turn.

4th Row: Knit to end.

5th Row: Knit 28, work SR, turn.

6th Row: Knit to end.

7th Row: Knit 26, work SR, turn.

8th Row: Knit to end.

Continue as above, working 2 sts less in every odd row until 4 sts remain.

Knit 2, work SR, turn, knit to end.

Knit 2 rows across all stitches.

Repeat SR sequence until 13 segments have been worked. Cast off and sew first segment to last segment using mattress stitch (see How To chapter).

Sew a row of gathering stitches around centre opening and draw up to close.

Make another circle for back of cushion.

DECORATIONS

Thread 30 cm (12 in) lengths of 'Lasagna' along the curves that separate the short row segments, leaving approximately 5 cm (2½ in) of yarn at the edge of the cushion and taking the other end through the centre hole to be stitched down later.

Weave another length under and over the first line of trim. Repeat for each segment.

Knot the two ends on the outside of each curve together.

Push all ends at the centre of the cushion through to the back and stitch each one down with a couple of stitches to secure.

Attach 12 cm (4½ in) lengths of 'Odyssey Glitz' to the centre of the cushion between each line of trim—I used one length per section but you can use more if you want.

CENTRE FLOWER

Ch 5, join with sl st into a circle.

1st Round: 12 dc(sc) into circle.

2nd Round: Work 5 tr(dc) in to each st around circle. Fasten off and stitch to centre of panel.

FINISHING

With WS together, work dc(sc) through both thicknesses, making sure that each curved segment line meets at the edges. When you get a little over halfway, insert the cushion blank and continue crocheting the seam together.

Spiral

This project comes under the 'altering the surface' category in that you use several different yarns, which are changed as and when you like and which break up the surface in a random manner. It's a freeform technique that is often used in a linear way to make bags and scarves.

This cushion is worked in the round, except that instead of joining each round to the beginning of the previous one you simply keep going round and round in a spiral until you reach the required diameter.

This can make it difficult to know just where each round ends, so it's a good idea to mark the end of the very first round with a pin or stitch marker.

Fig 117

The other thing you have to watch is the increasing. In general you need to follow the basic geometry of a circle and use the correct increasing formula (see below), but depending on the yarns used this can change in any given round, in which case the increasing can become more sporadic. This tends to happen if you are using a thick yarn along with several finer yarns as was the case with my cushion. See the increasing tips listed below.

You can use any stitch you like to make the cushion; however, if you use one of the taller stitches such as a treble (double crochet) it's a good idea to taper the beginning and end of the spiral with some graduated shorter stitches in order to prevent a 'stepped' effect.

Basic increasing formula

1st Round: no increases; if using tr(dc) work 12 sts into starting ring.

2nd Round: increase in every stitch.

3rd Round: increase in every 2nd stitch.

4th Round: increase in every 3rd stitch.

5th Round: increase in every 4th stitch.

6th Round: increase in every 5th stitch.

And so on until circle diameter is reached.

Tips on increasing

You will need to use your own judgement as to how many increases are required in any given round after the first few rounds have been completed and especially if you are using a heavier yarn along with the finer ones. It's quite easy to see what's happening, as the circle will start to 'ruffle' if you are increasing more than you need, and will begin to take on a cup shape if you aren't increasing often enough. One thing I keep a watch for is a stitch that starts to lean away from where the next stitch is to go—this generally means you need to increase a stitch at that position.

Notes

Gauge is not important for this project.

Where you choose to change yarns is up to you and thus there are no specific instructions for yarn changes.

YOU WILL NEED

100 g (3½ oz) Cleckheaton 'Country' 8-ply

1 ball Plymouth Yarns 'Patches'

1 ball Plymouth Yarns 'Noch Eros'

1 ball Plymouth Yarns 'Parrot'

6 mm (J/10) crochet hook

1 x 30 cm (12 in) cushion insert

wool needle

one decorative button for cushion centre

INSTRUCTIONS

Change yarns as you like—there is no set rule as to how many stitches or rounds of any one colour should be used.

1st Round: Make a circle using the loop method (see How To chapter), work 1 ch to secure loop, 1 dc(sc), 1 htr(hdc) and 10 tr(dc) into loop. Pull long tail to close circle, place marker into last stitch of round but do not join to first stitch. Continue as follows:

2nd Round: Into first st of previous round work 2 tr(dc), then 2 tr(dc) into each stitch around (24 sts), move marker.

3rd Round: Into first st work 2 tr(dc), *miss one st, 2 tr(dc) into next stitch, rep from * to end of round.

Continue working round and round, changing colours and increasing as needed until the circle measures the required diameter for your cushion insert.

Work another circle using just the plain yarn, this time following the increasing instructions as given.

FINISHING

I like to crochet decorative cushion panels together as it makes it easier to undo them for washing if required.

With wrong sides together work a row of dc(sc) right on the edge of the panels through both thicknesses, leaving an opening big enough to fit the cushion insert through. Insert the cushion and continue closing the seam.

Sew button to centre of the cushion.

Fig 118

YOU WILL NEED

150 g (5½ oz) Cleckheaton 'Country' 8-ply

1 ball Plymouth Yarns 'Odyssey Glitz'

5.5 mm (US9) needles

15 mm (US19) needles

5 mm (USH/8) crochet hook

30 cm (12 in) cushion insert

96 size 11 beads in colours to match decorative panel

beading thread

sewing needle to fit through beads

Gauge: 17 sts and 32 rows per 10 cm (4 in) measured over garter stitch.

INSTRUCTIONS

CUSHION PANELS
Make 2.

Cast on 50 sts in 8-ply and knit in garter stitch until panel measures 29 cm (11¼ in). Cast off loosely.

OVERLAY
With size 15 mm (US19) needles cast on 10 sts in 'Odyssey Glitz' and work 18 rows st st. Cast off.

Position overlay 6 cm (2½ in) from the bottom of the front panel and stretch it slightly so that the opposite edge lies along the ridge between rows 21 and 22, counted from the top of the panel. Pin into place. Using a small running stitch sew overlay in place around all edges.

ADDING BEADS
Following instructions for straight line bead back stitch (see How To chapter), sew three beads at a time along the edges of the overlay about 1.5 cm (½ in) apart.

FINISHING
With right sides together work dc(sc) through both thicknesses around three sides of the cushion. Place cushion insert inside and continue crocheting the final seam.

Sari Mesh

YOU WILL NEED

4 x 50 g (1¾ oz) balls Cleckheaton 'Country' 8-ply

1 x 100 g (3½ oz) hank Himalaya Yarn 'Sari Silk'

36 cm (14 in) cushion insert

4 mm (US6) knitting needles

5 mm (USH) crochet hook

wool needle

Fig 119

Gauge: 22 sts and 30 rows to 10 cm (4 in) using size 4 mm (US6) knitting needles and 8-ply yarn.

INSTRUCTIONS

BASE FABRIC
Make two.

Cast on 80 sts in 8-ply and knit 110 rows in stocking stitch.

Cast off loosely.

SARI SILK OVERLAY
Chain 36 + 9 for turning chain (10 spaces).

Row 1: 1 dc(sc) in 9th ch from hook, *5 ch, miss 3 ch, dc(sc) in next ch, rep from * to end, 5 ch, turn.

Row 2: *dc(sc) in centre of 5 ch, 5 ch, rep from * ending with dc(sc) in 6th ch of turning ch, 5 ch, turn.

Row 3: *dc(sc) in centre of 5 ch, 5 ch, rep from * to end, 5 ch, turn.

Repeat row 3 for pattern until 25 rows have been worked. Fasten off.

FINISHING
Block and steam one base section to size. While it is still pinned in place on the blocking board, place the overlay on top and stretch it to fit the background. Pin in place.

Using a small running stitch and Sari Silk, sew the overlay to the background through the very edge stitches, as close as you can to the edge of the background fabric.

With WS together and using the 8-ply yarn, crochet around three edges using dc(sc) and working at least 3 dc(sc) into each corner. Place cushion insert inside and continue crocheting the final edge.

When you reach the end, fasten off leaving a 10 cm (4 in) tail. Tie a little piece of contrasting yarn to the tail and then run the tail along the seam inside the back panel, making sure that a little bit of the contrast is still visible. When the time comes to wash the cushion you'll know exactly where the crocheted seam ends, making it easier to undo the seam and remove the insert.

Shawls

Fly Away shawl

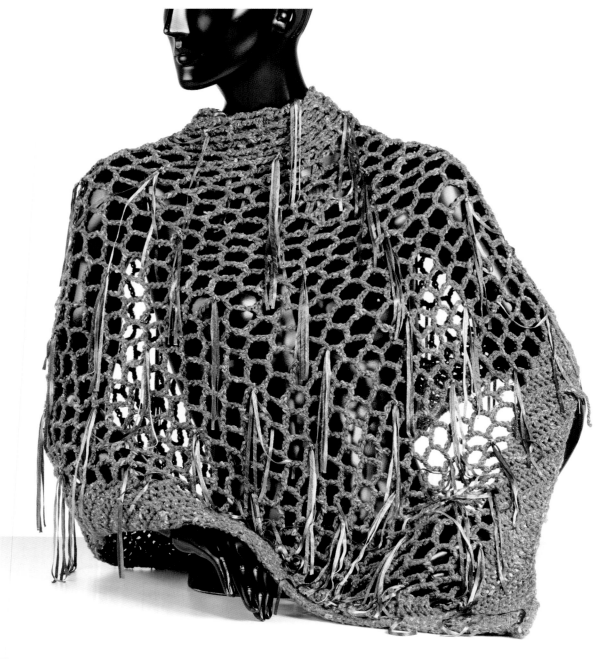

Fig 120

This shawl was inspired by two baby peewees, birds which are native to Australia, who started life in a large gum tree which is growing in our neighbour's yard, right up against the dividing fence. I found one baby on my driveway one morning, desperately trying to fly but unable to do so. My neighbour and I were able to rescue it and put it back in the tree but for days I worried about it. And sure enough a few days later there it was again, even further down my backyard, sitting in a palm tree just above ground level—or perhaps it was the sibling on this occasion. This time I think it had actually flown down from the tree but was unable to generate enough wing-power to fly back home. Fortunately, although obviously nervous and squawking loudly, it allowed me to pick it up and restore it to its tree, this time with my husband's help. For the next few days I kept a watchful eye on both babies from my studio window but fortunately no more rescues were required.

One morning I heard a great deal of parent and baby bird noises and looked out to see one of the parents madly flapping its wings while a baby copied the action. Obviously a flying lesson from a desperate parent worn out from constantly having to bring food home to two chicks! From that day on the chicks started moving around the branches, graduating from tiny little fluttering leaps to actual short flights, so that it became harder and harder for me to find them among the leaves. One day I saw both parents and both chicks on my back lawn having a 'worm catching' lesson, so I knew that a finally the chicks had 'earned their wings'. As I watched the lesson, both parents suddenly flew off, followed just seconds later by the babies. Freedom at last!

I continue to monitor the progress of this little family but as each day passes the chicks are getting more and more independent. One day they will leave home to create their own families but in the meantime they are giving me a whole lot of pleasure and in return I dedicate this shawl to them.

I chose not to use black and white, the actual colours of these birds, instead using the colours of the gum tree in which they started life's journey. The ribbons signify the flapping wings of a young bird as it discovers the freedom of flight and the fluttering of the gum leaves in a summer breeze.

You will need

300 g (10½ oz) Cleckheaton 'Country Silk' #8

50 g (1¾ oz) Anny Blatt ribbon # 268

50 g (1¾ oz) Anny Blatt ribbon # l570

6.50 mm (K/10½) crochet hook

Gauge is not critical for this shawl.

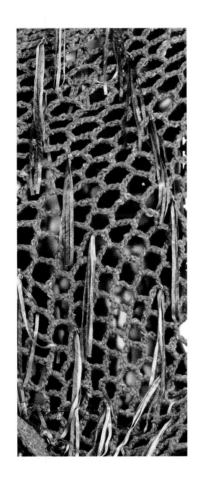

INSTRUCTIONS

Make 2 ch.

Base Row: 1 htr(hdc) into 2nd ch from hook, turn.

1st Row: 2 ch, 2 htr(hdc) into next htr(hdc), turn.

2nd Row: 2 ch, 2 htr(hdc) into each of next 2 htr(hdc), turn (4 htr/hdc).

3rd Row: 2 ch, 2 htr(hdc) into next htr(hdc), 1 htr(hdc) into each of next 2 htr(hdc), 2 htr(hdc) into last htr(hdc), turn (6 htr/hdc).

4th Row: 2 ch, 2 htr(hdc) into next htr(hdc), 1 htr(hdc) into each of next 4 htr(hdc), 2 htr(hdc) into last htr(hdc), turn (8 htr/hdc).

5th to 14th Rows: Continue to inc 1 htr(hdc) at each end of every row until there are 26 htr(hdc), turn.

15th Row: 3 ch to count as first tr(dc), 2 tr(dc) into first tr(dc), 1 tr(dc) into each of next 11 sts, 5 ch, miss 2 tr(dc), 1 tr(dc) in each of next 11 sts, 3 tr(dc) into top of turning ch, turn.

16th Row: 3 ch to count as first tr(dc), 2 tr (dc) into first tr(dc), 1 tr(dc) into each of next 11 sts, 5 ch, miss 2 tr(dc), 1 tr(dc) in 5ch sp, 5 ch, miss 2 tr(dc), 1 tr(dc) in each of next 11 sts, 3 tr(dc) in top of turning ch, turn.

17th Row: 3 ch to count as first tr(dc), 2 tr (dc) into first tr(dc), 1 tr(dc) into each of next 11 sts, 5 ch, miss 2 tr, *1 tr in 5ch sp, 5 ch*, rep from * to * once, miss 2 tr(dc), 1 tr(dc) into each of next 11 sts, 3 tr(dc) in top of turning ch, turn.

18th Row: 3 ch to count as first tr(dc), 2 tr (dc) into first tr(dc), 1 tr(dc) into each of next 11 sts, 5 ch, miss 2 tr, *1 tr in 5ch sp, 5 ch*, rep from * to * twice, miss 2 tr(dc), 1 tr(dc) into each of next 11 sts, 3 tr(dc) in top of turning ch, turn.

Rep the last row, working from * to * three times in the 19th row, four times in the 20th row, increasing one space in each row until there are 46 spaces.

Next Row: 1 ch, 1 dc(sc) in each of next 14 tr(dc), *3 dc in 5ch sp, 1 dc(sc) in next tr(dc). Rep from * 44 times, ending with 3 dc(sc) in last 5ch sp, 1 dc(sc) in each tr(dc) to end, 1 dc(sc) in top of turning ch. Fasten off.

TO DECORATE

Cut ribbons into 30 cm (12 in) lengths and attach them over the surface of the shawl.

Freda's shawl

Freda is my friend Sue's mother and she's made many of these shawls.
This one she made for Sue, who gave it to me to 'adorn'.

Fig 121

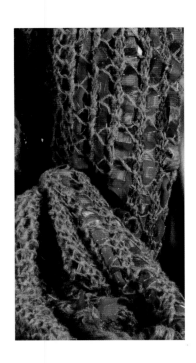

YOU WILL NEED

200 g (7 oz) very fine mohair

20 mm (US19) knitting needles

chiffon fabric or something similar for weaving (it should be a fabric that will rip easily)

INSTRUCTIONS

Cast on a multiple of 3 sts; for a shawl the same width as Freda's, you will need 75 sts.

1st Row: k1, yfwd, k2tog.

Repeat this row until shawl measures 245 cm (97 in) or length required.

Cut 30 cm (12 in) lengths of yarn and loop several strands together through ends of shawl for fringe.

Tear fabric into strips approximayely 2.5 cm (1 in) wide and weave through fabric, leaving long tails to form part of fringing.

Easy Adornments

Here are just a few ideas for making jewellery that can be used as neck adornments or closures for plain garments, as well as stand-alone jewellery.

It may not be possible to find the exact same trims as I've used in the neckpieces but a leisurely stroll through your local haberdashery or craft shops will provide many other alternatives. If you have access to the Internet, a search for 'creative trims' will also provide lots of possibilities.

Rhinestone neckpiece

YOU WILL NEED

25 g (1 oz) black 8-ply yarn

optional: 5 cm (20 in) Plymouth 'Electra' or narrow ribbon

3 mm (D/3) crochet hook

beads: an assortment of black, white, clear and silver-lined seed beads, sizes 8 and 11

rhinestone trim (see Resources)

craft glue

sewing thread and needle to fit through bead holes

Gauge is not important for this project.

Fig 122

INSTRUCTIONS

STRAP

Make 3 ch.

1st Row: Miss 1 ch, 1 dc(sc) in next 2 ch, 1 ch, turn.

2nd Row: 1 dc(sc) in each st, 1 ch, turn.

Rep 2nd row until strap measures 72 cm (28 in).

DECORATIVE ELEMENTS

I've used a freeform approach to make this neckpiece and you can choose to follow my ideas as roughly explained below, or use your own. It's great fun to just keep adding things as the ideas come to you. You may have trouble finding a similar rhinestone trim to the one I have used on the strap and if so you can substitute another similar one or use little buttons.

Once you have made the strap, stitch the last 2 cm (¾ in) together, making sure that it isn't twisted.

CENTRAL FLOWER

Make 4 ch and join with a sl st to form ring.

1st Round: (RS) [4 ch, 3 dtr(tr), 4 ch, sl st] into ring 5 times. Fasten off leaving a 10 cm (4 in) tail.

Fill centre of flower with beads or use a small decorative button.

Sew flower to joined section of strap.

Cut 6 rhinestone flowers from the trim and glue to each side of the strap as shown in the photograph.

DANGLES

Attach 8-ply yarn to lower edge of strap, ch 12, work 1 dc(sc) into 4th ch from hook (ring formed). Into ring work 3 ch then 6 tr(dc), join with sl st to top of 3 ch (bobble formed). Chain a further 8 ch or so. Fasten off.

SMALL FLOWER

With #4 cotton make 3 ch, join with sl st into a circle.

1st Round: 8 dc(sc) into circle, join with sl st to first dc(sc).

2nd Round: *4 ch, dc(sc) in next dc(sc), rep from * 7 more times, ending with sl st into base of first 4 ch.

3rd Round: 5 dc(sc) into each 4ch loop, fasten off.

LEAVES
Make 2.

Using 8-ply make 10 ch.

1st Row: 1 dc(sc) into 2nd ch from hook, 1 dc(sc) in next ch, 1 htr(hdc) in next ch, 1 tr(dc) in next 3 ch, 1 htr(hdc) in next ch, 1 dc(sc) in next ch, sl st in last ch, fasten off.

Attach small flower and two leaves to end of chain extending from the bobble. Glue rhinestone flower or sew a little button to flower centre.

TINY ROUND FLOWER
Using 8-ply yarn make 4 ch, join with sl st into a circle.

1st Round: 8 dc(sc) into circle.

2nd Round: 2 dc(sc) in each dc(sc) around circle, join with sl st to first dc(sc), 8 ch, fasten off leaving a 12 cm (4½ in) tail. Stitch dangle to bottom RH corner of strap. Glue rhinestone flower to centre of flower.

BEAD DANGLES
Attach thread to bottom of strap behind the main flower. Thread 8–10 cm (3–4 in) of beads randomly onto fine crochet cotton or beading thread, miss last 2 or 3 beads and take the thread back up the rest of the beads. Secure to edge of strap. Repeat for as many bead dangles as you require

OPTIONAL
Attach tassel consisting of several ends of a similar yarn to the one I've used, Plymouth 'Electra', which is a fine thread with tiny tufts every 6 mm (¼ in) or so. Or you could use a shiny ribbon which will add another texture.

You may find that the flower dangles will want to twist backwards, but when you are wearing it the piece will hang properly.

Fig 123

YOU WILL NEED

small amount of 8-ply yarn

1 m (40 in) zigzag trim in suitable colour (I've used one called Uni-trim which I found in a craft store)

2.5 mm (C/2) crochet hook

sewing needle

sewing thread

INSTRUCTIONS

Make 5 ch, turn.

1st Row: Miss 1 ch, dc(sc) in next 4 ch, 1 ch, turn.

2nd Row: 1 dc(sc) in each dc(sc), 1 ch, turn.

3rd Row: 2 dc(sc) in first dc(sc), 1 dc(sc) in each dc(sc) to end, 1 ch, turn.

4th Row: 1 dc(sc) in each dc(sc) to end.

Rep rows 3 and 4until you have 10 sts.

Work 1 row dc(sc).

Dec on next and each alternate row until 6 sts remain.

Work 5 rows.

Increase on next and each alternate row until you have 12 sts.

Continue for strap:

Work 2 dc(sc), 1 ch, turn.

Rep this row until strap measures 72 cm (28 in). Fasten off and stitch to the other side of main piece.

Using a small straight stitch, sew braid to neckpiece, starting in the lower RH corner and finishing in the lower LH edge.

Spangles necklace

What wonderful little 'bits' the paillettes used in this project are! They come in a variety of shapes, in all the colours of the rainbow, and are as light as a feather, making them perfect for adding to knitted or crocheted fabrics. (Paillettes are available from Trendsetter Yarns—see Resources.)

Fig 124

YOU WILL NEED

1 box lilac chips (20 pieces)

1 box khaki ovals (20 pieces); on the necklace in the photograph the
ovals have been sorted into graduating sizes, with the smaller ones
used at either end

small amount 4-ply Clever Country cotton with gold thread #2180 (see
Resources)

2.5 mm (C/2) hook

1 x 1 cm (½ in) button

INSTRUCTIONS

Make 121 ch.

1st Row: 1 dc(sc) in 2nd ch from hook, dc(sc) to end, 1 ch, turn.

2nd Row: 1 dc(sc) in next 20 sts, 1 htr(hdc) in next 21 sts, *5 ch, insert
hook into a chip, draw thread through chip and the loop on the hook,
5 ch, sl st into 10th ch from hook, 1 htr(hdc) in next st, *5 ch, insert
hook into an oval, draw thread through oval and the loop on the hook,
5 ch, sl st in 10th ch from hook, 1 htr(hdc) in next st.

Continue in this manner, alternating chips and ovals 18 more times.
Work from * to * once.

Complete the other side of the strap by working 1 htr(hdc) in next 19
sts, 1 dc(sc) in next 20 sts. Do not fasten off.

Make loop closure: ch 6 and sl st to other side of the strap. Fasten off.

Sew button to other end of strap.

Aquamarine pin

This piece is used as the closure for the Aquamarine jacket (see page 153), and is therefore made with colours to complement that particular garment. You can of course substitute your own colours.

You will need

small amount of 8-ply yarn from Aquamarine jacket

size 4 mm (US6) knitting needles

size 4 mm crochet hook

1 x 63 mm (2 ½ in) kilt pin

1 x 2.5 cm (1 in) rubber O-ring or curtain ring

12 x 6 mm (¼ in) aqua glass or plastic beads, preferably with holes large enough to slide over yarn

off-cut of bead fringing

OR beads to make fringing:

      110 x 2 mm metallic bugle beads

      13 x 3 mm pink or purple clear beads

      3 x 1 cm (½ in) clear tube beads

      3 red teardrop beads

      beading thread and needle to fit through bead holes

Instructions

Special abbreviation

bdc(bsc)—bead double crochet/bead single crochet (see How To chapter)

Cast on 6 sts.

Work in moss st for 12 cm (4¾ in). Cast off.

Making sure that the pin opening is at the top right, fold approximately 1 cm (½ in) of knitted background over the non-opening bar of the pin and stitch down.

Thread aqua beads onto yarn and work 24 bdc(bsc) around O-ring, join with sl st to first dc(sc). (If the bead holes aren't big enough for yarn to fit through, skip this instruction and sew the beads to the circle later.) Fasten off and sew the ring to the background about 1.5 cm (¾ in) below the pin bar.

BEAD TASSEL

If using an off-cut of purchased bead tassel, sew at least 3 drops to the background underneath the ring.

If making your own, thread beads onto beading thread as follows: 9 bugles, 1 clear 3 mm, 2 pink 3 mm, 1 clear 3 mm, 6 bugles, 1 x 3 mm, 1 tube, 1 x 3 mm, 6 bugles, 2 x 3 mm, 4 bugles, 1 x 3 mm, 4 bugles, 1 teardrop, 1 bugle. Miss last bugle and take thread back up all the beads to the top. Sew a couple of stitches to secure the drop.

Repeat for two more drops, alternating the beads as required.

Fig 125

Natural Stone pin

This pin doesn't use knitting or crochet unless you want it to. Using craft felt is just another way of making a very quick closure or piece of jewellery. The fun part about these pin closures is that you can use just about anything you want as the decorative elements. I've given you a list of what I used but since you may not be able to find the exact same things, substitutions will be necessary. I suggest trips to thrift and secondhand shops—they are a great source of found-object treasures and I can highly recommend taking the time to do it.

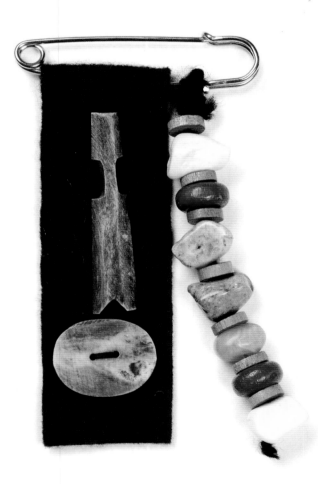

YOU WILL NEED

2.5 x 11 cm (1 x 4½ in) strip of black craft felt

1 x 63 mm (2½ in) kilt pin

faux bone accent beads or buttons

mix of wood and stone-coloured beads, with large holes if possible

60 cm (24 in) length of 8-ply yarn; if your beads don't have large holes you will need to use a finer yarn

3 mm (US5) hook

INSTRUCTIONS

Stitch accent beads or buttons to felt strip. Fold over a 1 cm (½ in) hem and stitch down over the non-opening bar of the pin, making sure that the pin opening is at the top right.

Leaving a 10 cm (4 in) tail, make 5 or 6 ch with the length of yarn, pull yarn through last loop to close the chain length, then thread 10 cm (4 in) of beads in any arrangement you like onto the long end. Make a double knot after the last bead, making sure it's secure. You may like to add a drop of Fray Check for added security.

Stitch the short chain length over the pin bar and fasten securely. Trim end and add a little Fray Check if desired.

Fig 126

Rainbow Ringlets

Another fun find while browsing through my local two-dollar shop recently was a collection of colourful pony-tail rings, not something I would normally buy since I have short hair and no daughters! But what fabulous colours for a fun piece of jewellery.

Fig 127

You will need

small amount of 8-ply yarn

4 mm (US7) crochet hook

6 pony-tail rings

1 kilt pin

Instructions

Make 6 ch.

Base Row: 1 dc(sc) in 2nd ch from hook, dc(sc) to end, 1 ch, turn.

1st Row: 1 dc(sc) in each st to end, 1 ch, turn.

2nd Row: As 1st row.

3rd Row: 1 dc(sc) in first 2 sts, hold pony-tail ring at front of work, place hook through ring and into the 3rd stitch, draw yarn through the stitch and the ring so that there are two loops on the hook with the pony-tail ring trapped behind one loop, draw yarn through.

Work 3 rows of dc(sc) and then repeat 3rd row once.

Continue working these last four rows until you have used all 6 pony-tail rings.

Work 4 more rows of dc(sc). Fasten off leaving a 10 cm (4 in) tail.

Making sure that the pin opening is at the top right, fold the last 3 rows over the non-opening bar of the pin and stitch down. Sew in all ends.

Flower pin with beaded centre

YOU WILL NEED

approx. 2 m (2 yds) yarn left over from the Topaz top (see page 159)

small amounts of two contrast yarns

30 size 8 beads to complement contrast yarns

4 mm or 5 mm (F/5) crochet hook

1 pin back

beading thread and needle to fit through bead holes

Fig 128 (Optional adornment for Topaz —see page 159)

INSTRUCTIONS

Make two flowers as follows using the contrast yarns.

Make 6 ch, join with a sl st to form a circle.

1st Round: 3 ch, 2 tr(dc) into circle, [7 ch, 3 tr(dc) into circle] 4 times, 7 ch, 1 sl st into 3rd of 3 ch.

2nd Round: 3 ch, [miss 1 tr(dc), 1 tr(dc) into next tr(dc), 15 dtr(tr) into 7ch loop, 1 tr(dc) into next tr(dc)] 4 times, miss 1 tr(dc), 1 tr(dc) in next tr(dc), 15 dtr(tr) in 7ch loop, sl st to top of 3 ch. Fasten off.

Repeat for second flower.

Sew beads to centre of each flower.

Using a little of the yarn used for the Topaz top, make 4 ch, 1 dc(sc) into 2nd ch from hook, dc(sc) to end, 1 ch, turn.

Work rows of dc(sc) until piece measures 9 cm (3½ in), fasten off.

Sew flowers to either end of this strip through the centre and through the top edge of a petal to stop them drooping.

Centre the pin back at the top edge of strip and stitch into place.

Wristlet 1

To wear over a shirt cuff or as a bracelet.

YOU WILL NEED
10 g 8-ply Cleckheaton 'Country Naturals'

4 mm (US6) knitting needles

1 x 4 cm (1½ in) faux ivory oval bead

2 x 1 cm (½ in) beads to complement centre bead

Gauge is not important for this project.

INSTRUCTIONS
Cast on 12 sts and knit in garter stitch until work equals your wrist measurement.

Cast off and join to other end.

Attach beads as shown in the photograph.

If necessary, to help the beads lie flat sew a couple of couching stitches between the oval and round beads.

Fig 129

Wristlet 2

YOU WILL NEED

small amount of 8-ply (DK) yarn in colour of your choice

5 mm (US8) knitting needles

1 x loom flower (if you don't have a Knitwit Loom or Daisy Wheel [see
    Toys of the Trade chapter], you can use a crochet or knit flower from
    the Collage chapter)

Gauge is not important for this project.

INSTRUCTIONS

Cast on 14 sts and knit in cross stitch pattern (see Textured Stitches
chapter) until work equals your wrist measurement. Cast off and join
seam using mattress stitch (see How To chapter).

If you have a Knitwit Loom or Daisy Wheel, follow the manufacturer's
instructions to make one flower. If you don't have these tools you can
knit or crochet a flower or embellish your wristlet any way you like.

Sew flower/embellishments to centre of wristlet.

> *It is better to fail in
> originality than to succeed
> in imitation.*
>
> HERMAN MELVILLE

Fig 130

Jackets and Tops

Garnet jacket

A 'grow as you go' project.

YOU WILL NEED

15 x 50 g (1¾ oz) balls of Cleckheaton 'Country' 8-ply (if you want sleeves you will need a further 5 or 6 balls)

3 balls of fancy yarns, such as 'railway track' yarns, that can be easily pierced by the knitting needle

knitting needles (see note below)

GAUGE AND KNITTING NEEDLES

This jacket is made using my favourite method of constructing a garment, the 'grow as you go' method, and although gauge isn't totally necessary for this freeform approach, I used 17 sts to 10 cm (4 in) over garter stitch using 5 mm (US8) needles. I didn't use a row gauge, as it's an easy matter to stop knitting when you reach the length you want.

MEASUREMENT

My garment measures 116 cm (46 in) around and is 72 cm (28 in) long at the back and 68 cm (27 in) long at the front (this difference is intentional).

My panels were either 15 sts (9 cm/3 ½ in) or 20 sts (11 cm/4¼ in) wide. I used 2 narrow and one wide for each front and 4 narrow and 2 wide for the back. How you arrange them is up to you.

To determine the size of a jacket for yourself, choose a garment from your wardrobe that is a good fit.

Measure the fronts and the back of the garment at their widest points. The total measurement is what you divide into panels. The width of each panel will depend on the total measurement and the look you as the designer, wants. Narrow or wide, or a combination, it's entirely up to you.

You can use a pre-determined gauge to work out the number of stitches required for each panel or you can cast on x number of stitches, knit a few rows of the panel and then measure it. Deduct its measurement from the total front measurement and use it to determine how many stitches you will need for the next panel and so on. For example, I used 15 sts for the narrow panels and 20 sts for the wide panels, which worked out just fine.

If you want to add sleeves you can work in the same way, but to make the sleeve narrower at the wrist (if that's the look you want), you should start with quite narrow strips and increase gradually to the width required.

INSTRUCTIONS

I worked in garter stitch with a special edging to faciliate the joining of the panels, and worked randomly spaced rows of fancy yarns using the fluffle stitch technique (see Textured Stitches chapter), the occasional small block of moss stitch or stocking stitch, and now and again a row of eyelets. When the panels were done I added various textured embellishments such as garter stitch triangles, moss stitch tabs, embroidery and so on. And of course you can add beads if you want!

SPECIAL EDGING FOR GARTER STITCH PANELS

Cast on required number of stitches.

At beginning of next and every row work the first stitch as follows:

slip one p-wise, take yarn back to knit position and knit to end of row.

This forms a chain stitch similar to a crocheted chain along each side of the panel. To join the panels you work dc(sc) through each stitch. I've used the ridged side as the right side for my garment (see Fig 131b) but if you were to join the panels using a contrast yarn, the other side gives a rather nice effect too.

Fig 131b

Aquamarine jacket

Note: Before starting this project, please refer to 'A word about options …' at the beginning of the project chapter.

FINISHED BUST MEASUREMENTS
Allowing approximately 5–10 cm (2–4 in) of ease.

	Metric	Imperial
XS	85.5	34¼
S	96.75	38¾
M	108	43¼
L	119	47½
1X	130	52
2X	141	56½
3X	152	61

Fig 132a

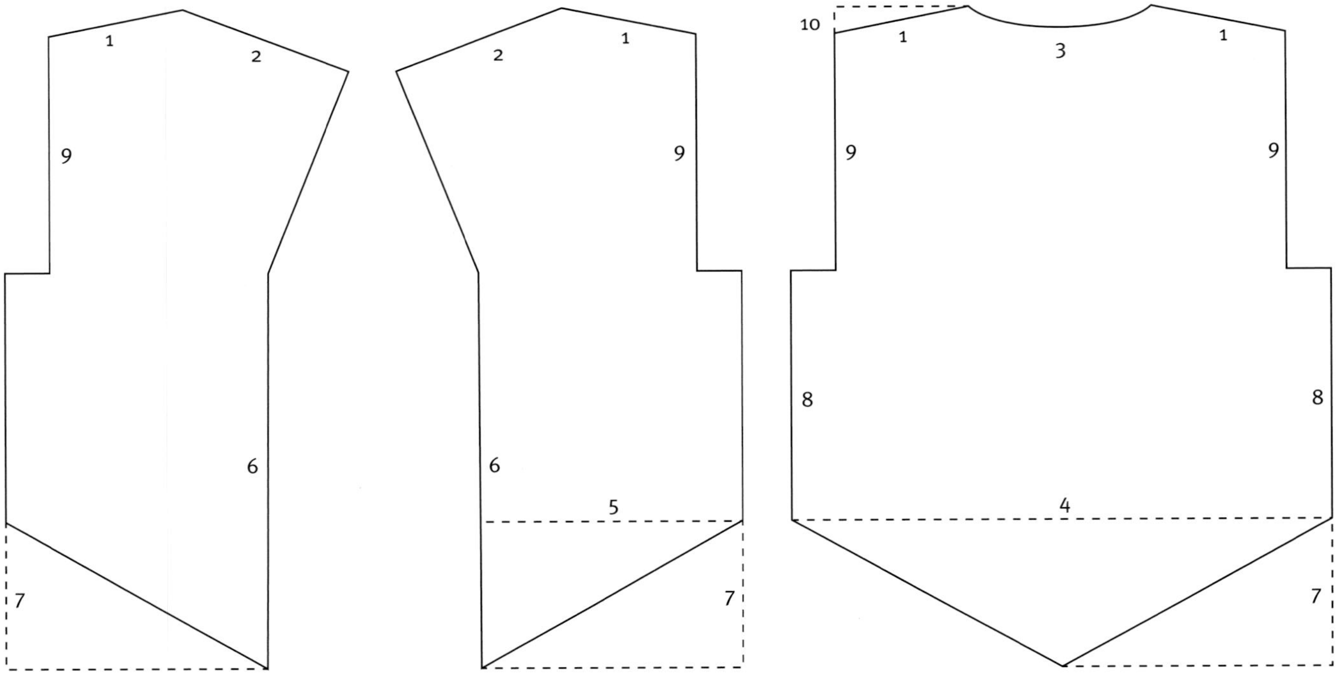

Fig 132b

#1 is shoulder width for back and front shoulders
11.75 (13.25, 15, 16.75, 18.25, 20, 21.75) cm
4¾ (5¼, 6, 6¾, 7¼, 8, 8¾) inches

#2 is width of the front collar folded over section
14.5 (15, 16, 17.75, 18.25, 20, 20.5) cm
5¾ (6, 6½, 7, 7¼, 8, 8¼) inches

#3 is back neck width
12.25 (13.25, 14.5, 16.75, 17.75, 20, 21) cm
5 (5¼, 5¾, 6¾, 7, 8, 8½) inches

#4 is widest width of back
42.25 (47.75, 53.25, 59, 64.5, 70, 75.5) cm
17 (19, 21¼, 23½, 25¾, 28, 30¼) inches

#5 is widest part of the fronts
21.75 (24.5, 27.25, 30, 32.75, 35.50, 38.25) cm
8¾ (9¾, 11, 12, 13, 14¼, 15¼) inches

#6 is total length from tip of the points to underarm
43.75 (45, 45, 46.25, 46.25, 47.5, 47.5) cm
17½ (18, 18, 18½, 18½, 19, 19) inches

#7 is length of front and back from tip of point to end of the shaping of the point
11.75 (13.25, 15, 16.75, 18.25, 20, 21.75) cm
4¾ (5¼, 6, 6¾, 7¼, 8, 8¾) inches

#8 is length of side seam for front and back
32 (31.75, 30, 29.5, 28, 27.5, 25.75) cm
12¾ (12¾,12,11¾, 11¼, 11, 10¼) inches

#9 is armhole depth for fronts and back
26 (26.5, 27, 28, 28, 28.5, 28.5) cm
10¼ (10½, 10¾, 11¼, 11½, 11½) inches

#10 is shoulder shaping measurement
3.25 cm and 1¼ inches

Optional sleeves
#11 is sleeve length
47.5 (47.5, 49, 49, 51.25, 51.25) cm
19 (19, 19½, 19½, 20½, 20½) inches

#12 is sleeve cuff width
25.75 (26.75, 27.5, 31.25, 31.25, 32.5, 32.5) cm
10¼ (10¾, 11, 12½, 12½, 13, 13) inches

#13 is sleeve width at top
51.25 (52.5, 53, 57, 57, 57.5, 57.5) cm
20½ (21, 21¼, 22¾, 22¾, 23, 23) inches

YOU WILL NEED

8-ply (DK); I used Cleckheaton 'Country' 8-ply (see Resources):

> 8 (9, 10, 12, 13, 14, 16) 50 g (1¾ oz) balls

> or 765 (850, 950, 1090, 1190, 1325, 1430) metres

> or 800 (930, 1040, 1190, 1300, 1450, 1565) yards

optional sleeves require:

> 5 (5, 5, 5, 5, 6, 6) extra balls of the same yarn

> or 395 (410, 425, 465, 465, 485, 485) metres

> or 430 (445, 465, 510, 510, 50, 530) yards

5 mm (US8) knitting needles

5 mm (US8) circular needles for doing edges

Gauge: 18 sts 24 rows over 10 cm or 4 inches in st st.

Note: The yarn is worked at a looser than standard gauge which allows for more drape in the fabric.

INSTRUCTIONS

Back

Cast on 6 sts.

Starting on WS, purl 1 row.

Working in st st (knit 1 row, purl 1 row), *at beg of each of next 2 rows cast on 3 sts and work to end of row.

Next row: Cast on 2 sts at beg of next 2 rows*.

Repeat from * to * a total of 7 (8, 9, 10, 11, 12, 13) times, to reach 76 (86, 96, 106, 116, 126, 136) sts, ending with WS row.

Work even until back measures 43.75 (45, 45, 46.25, 46.25, 47.5, 47.5) cm or 17½ (18, 18, 18½, 18½, 19, 19) inches.

Shape armhole

At the beginning each of the next 2 rows, cast off 6 (7, 8, 8, 9, 9, 10) sts. Work even until armhole measures 26 (26.5, 27, 28, 28, 28.5, 28.5) cm or 10¼ (10½, 10¾, 11¼, 11¼, 11½, 11½) inches.

Shape shoulders

At beg of each of the next 4 rows, cast off 5 (6, 7, 7, 8, 9, 10) sts, *except* on fourth row, work to 11 (12, 13, 16, 17, 18, 19) sts on needle, and cast off the next 20 (20, 22, 26, 28, 30, 32) sts for back of neck and work to end of row. At the start of the next armhole edge row, cast off 5 (6, 7, 7,

8, 9, 10) sts and work to end of row. Turn. Cast off 1 (2, 2, 2, 2, 3, 3) sts at neck edge and work to end of row. Cast off remaining sts. Attach yarn at start of centre cast-off sts and purl to end of row. Cast off 5 (6, 7, 7, 8, 9, 10) sts and work to end of row. Turn. Cast off 1 (2, 2, 2, 2, 3, 3) sts at neck edge and work to end of row. Cast off remaining sts.

LEFT FRONT

Cast on 4 sts. Starting on WS, purl 1 row. Working in st st (knit 1 row, purl 1 row), *at beg of the next RS row, cast on 3 sts and work to end of row. Purl 1 row. Cast on 2 sts at beg of next RS row*.

Repeat from * to * a total of 7 (8, 9, 10, 11, 12, 13) times, to reach 39 (44, 49, 54, 59, 64, 69) sts. Work even until front measures 43.75 (45, 45, 46.25, 46.25, 47.5, 47.5) cm or 17½ (18, 18, 18½, 18½, 19, 19) inches, ending with WS row.

Shape armhole

At the beginning of the next RS row, cast off 6 (7, 8, 8, 9, 9, 10) sts and work to end of row. Work 1 row even.

Shape collar and shoulder

On RS, work to 1 st rem, inc 1 st in the next st, and repeat this increase every fourth row a total of 14 (14, 15, 16, 16, 17, 17) times. Work 4 rows even, and then at beg of every WS row, cast off 4 sts at neck edge 6 (6, 7, 8, 8, 9, 9) times, and at beg of next WS row cast off 2 (3, 1, 0, 1, 0, 1) sts while at the *same time*, when armhole measures the same as back, shaping shoulders by casting off 5 (6, 7, 7, 8, 9, 10) sts at armhole edge 3 times, and 6 (6, 6, 6, 9, 9, 9) sts once.

RIGHT FRONT

Cast on 4 sts. Starting on RS, knit 1 row. Working in st st (knit 1 row, purl 1 row), *at the beginning of the next WS row, cast on 3 sts and work to end of row. Knit 1 row. Then, cast on 2 sts at the beginning of next WS row*. Repeat from * to *for a total of 7 (8, 9, 10, 11, 12, 13) times to reach 39 (44, 49, 54, 59, 64, 69) sts.

Work until same length as left front, ending with RS row.

Shape armhole

At the beginning the next WS row, cast off 6 (7, 8, 8, 9, 9, 10) sts and work to end of row.

Shape collar and shoulder

On RS, increase 1 st at beginning of row and repeat this increase every 4th row a total of 14 (14, 15, 16, 16, 17, 17) times. Work 4 rows even, and then at the beginning of every RS row, cast off 4 sts at neck edge 6 (6, 7, 8, 8, 9, 9) times, and at beg of next RS row cast off 2 (3, 1, 0, 1,

0, 1) sts *while at the same time*, when the armhole measures same as back, shaping shoulders by casting off 5 (6, 7, 7, 8, 9, 10) sts at armhole edge 3 times, and 6 (6, 6, 6, 9, 9, 9) sts once.

OPTIONAL SLEEVES

Cast on 46 (48, 50, 56, 56, 58,58) sts. Work increases as for Ruby (page 166) to 92 (94, 96, 102, 104, 104) sts, to same lengths as for Ruby (page 166), and cast off.

FINISHING

Block and steam garment pieces.

Using mattress stitch (see How To chapter) sew shoulder and underarm seams

EDGING

You can proceed with your own edging if you prefer.

If you don't have circular needles or don't like using them, you can join the shoulders and then work the armhole edgings of your choice before sewing the underarm seams together.

With RS facing, work a row of dc(sc) around all edges. A good rule of thumb is to pick up every 2nd stitch on the vertical edges and every stitch on the horizontal edges, but do check your work every now and again to make sure it's not ruffling (too many stitches) or pulling in (not enough stitches).

With RS facing and using 4 mm (US6) circular needles, pick up and knit 2 rows of 1 x 1 rib all around armholes, lower edge and along the back neck and the top of the collar extensions. You can also add the rib to the front edges if you prefer, but I chose to let them roll.

EMBELLISHING OPTIONS

Normally the extension on this garment would fold back to make a lapel style of collar; since the garment is in stocking stitch, the reversed collar will show the purl face of the fabric. If you want the collar folded back it can be decorated using ideas from this book or left unadorned.

I rather liked the contemporary look created by crossing one front over the other and securing it with a specially created pin. See the Easy Adornments section (page 142) for instructions for making the pin shown in the photograph.

Topaz top

Who says that you need to decorate the surface of the garment! Why not create several neck adornments or special pins to wear with plain stocking stitch garments instead. See the Easy Adornments chapter for some ideas. Fig 133a shows a very easy way to dress up a plain top by using a reel of fancy trim that has been sewn together and then twisted to form a necklace. Fig 133b shows the same top with a decorative pin. Instructions for the decorative pin are on page 147.

Fig 133a Topaz top with braid trim used as a removable neck adornment

Before starting this project, please refer to 'A word about options ...' at the beginning of the project chapter.

FINISHED MEASUREMENTS

Allowing approximately 5–10 cm (2–4 in) of ease.

Bust		Base of neck to hem	
Metric	Imperial	Metric	Imperial
85	34	61.25	24½
95	38	61.25	24½
105	42	63.25	25¼
115	46	63.25	25¼
125	50	63.75	25½
135	54	65	26
145	58	65.75	26¼

YOU WILL NEED

8-ply (DK); I used Cleckheaton's 8-ply Crepe:

  7 (8, 9, 9, 10, 11, 12) 50 g (1¾ oz) balls

  or 620 (695, 790, 865, 950, 1040, 1130) metres

  or 680 (760, 865, 945, 1040, 1140, 1235) yards

5 mm (US8) needles

crochet hook or needles in size to suit the edging of your choice

Gauge: 18 sts x 24 rows over 10 cm (4 inches) worked in st st.

Note: The yarn for this garment was worked at a looser than standard gauge which allows for more drape in the fabric.

Because the fabric is stocking stitch the edges of this garment will roll.

INSTRUCTIONS

BACK AND FRONT

Cast on 77 (86, 95, 104, 113, 122, 131) sts. Starting on RS, work in st st (knit 1 row, purl 1 row) to 37.5 (37.5, 39, 39, 39, 40, 40) cm or 15 (15, 15½, 15½, 15½, 16, 16) inches, ending with a WS row.

Armhole shaping

Cast off 4 (5, 6, 6, 7, 7, 8) sts at beginning of next 2 rows. Then cast off 0 (0, 2, 2, 3, 3, 3) sts at the beginning of next 2 rows. Decrease 1 st at each end of every RS row 4 (6, 5, 7, 7, 10, 13) times to reach 61 (64, 69, 74, 79, 82, 83) sts. Work even until armhole measures 21.25 (21.25, 22, 22, 22.5, 22,5, 23.75) cm or 8½ (8½, 8¾, 8¾, 9, 9, 9¼) inches, ending with a WS row.

Fig 133b Topaz top with floral pin (see Fig 128)

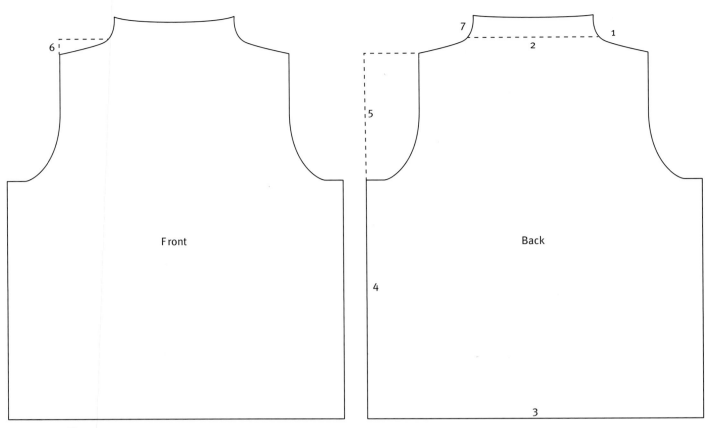

Fig 133c

#1 is shoulder width for back and front shoulders
8.25 (9, 9.5, 9.5, 10, 10.5, 11) cm
3¼ (3½, 3¾, 3¾, 4, 4¼, 4½) in

#2 is back neck width
19.5 (20, 21.75, 24.5, 26, 26.75, 26) cm
7¾ (8, 8¾, 9¾, 10½, 10¾, 10½) inches

#3 is bottom width of back and front
42.75 (47.75, 52.75, 57.75, 62.75, 67.75, 72.75) cm
17 (19, 21, 23, 25, 27, 29) inches

#4 is total length from bottom hem to underarm
37.5 (37.5, 39, 39, 39, 40, 40) cm
15 (15, 15½, 15½, 15½, 16, 16) inches

#5 is armhole depth from underarm to start of shoulders
21.25 (21.25, 22, 22, 22.5, 22.5, 23.75) cm
8½ (8½, 8¾, 8¾, 9, 9, 9½) inches

#6 is depth of shoulder shaping
2.5 cm
1 inch

#7 is funnel neck height
3.75 cm
1½ inches

Shoulder shaping

At the beginning of each of the next 4 rows, cast off 4 (5, 5, 5, 5, 6, 6) sts, then at the beginning of each of the next two rows cast off 5 (4, 5, 5, 6, 5, 6) sts.

Short row neck shaping:

At the beginning of each of the next 2 rows, decrease 1 st and then work in st st for 4 rows, repeat from * to * once.

Next row: *Work 5 sts, bring yarn to opposite side of fabric, slip 1 st, return yarn to original position, and slip the 1 st slipped back to the left needle and turn. Work to end of row*. Turn and work 1 row, then repeat from * to *. Cast off all stitches.

Work two pieces the same.

FINISHING

Block and steam garment pieces.

Sew all seams together using Mattress Stitch (see How To chapter)

When sewing the roll neck seam leave approx 2.5 cm (1 in) at the top and sew this section with the wrong sides together so that the seam is hidden.

EDGING

You can proceed with your own edging if you prefer.

If you don't have circular needles or don't like using them, you can join the shoulders and then work the armhole edgings of your choice before sewing the underarm seams together.

With circular needles, pick up and knit 4 rows of moss stitch around lower edges and armholes.

Note: If you are adding a crochet edging you may need to adjust stitches to ensure the correct multiple of stitches. This is easier to do while working the row of double crochet at the beginning of the pattern.

Work the crochet edging around the lower edges of the garment as follows:

Worked over a multiple of 8ch plus 2

1st Row: (WS) 1dc(sc) into 2nd ch from hook, 1dc(sc) into each ch to end, turn

2nd Row: 1ch, 1dc(sc) into next dc(sc), *3ch, miss next 3dc(sc), 3tr(dc) into next dc(sc), turn, 5ch, miss 2 tr(dc) sl st into next tr(dc), turn, 1ch, 7 dc(sc) into next 5ch sp, 3ch, miss next 3dc(sc), 1dc(sc) into next dc(sc), rep from * to end. Fasten off.

Ruby jacket

Before starting this project, please refer to 'A word about options …' at the beginning of the project chapter.

Fig 134a

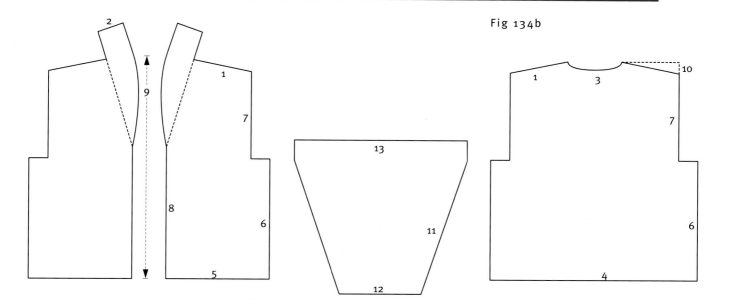

Fig 134b

#1 is shoulder width for back and front shoulders
11.75 (14, 15.5, 17.75, 20, 22.25) cm
4¾ (5½, 6¼, 7, 8, 9) inches

#2 is width of front collar – approx
10 cm or 4 inches for all sizes

#3 is back neck width
15.5 (15.5, 16.75, 16.75, 16.75, 17.75) cm
6¼ (6¼, 6¾, 6¾, 6¾, 7) inches

#4 is bottom width of back
47.75 (52.25, 57.75, 62.25, 67.75, 73.25) cm
19 (21, 23, 25, 27, 29¼) inches

#5 is bottom width of fronts
24.5 (26.75, 29.5, 31.75, 34.5, 37.25) cm
9¾ (10¾, 11¾, 12¾, 13¾, 15) inches

#6 is total length to underarm – back and fronts
37.5 (37.5, 38.75, 38.75, 40, 40) cm
15 (15, 15½, 15½, 16, 16) inches

#7 is armhole depth for fronts and back
25 (25, 26.25, 26.25, 27.5, 27.5) cm
10 (10, 10½, 10½, 11, 11) inches

#8 is front edge from hem to start of collar shaping
45 (45, 46.25, 46.25, 47.5, 47.5) cm
18 (18, 18½, 18½, 19, 19) inches

#9 is front edge to top of shoulder at collar edge
20.5 (20.5, 22, 22, 23, 23) cm
8¼ (8¼, 8¾, 8¾, 9¼, 9¼) inches

#10 is shoulder shaping measurement
3.25 cm or 1¼ inches

#11 is sleeve length
47.5 (47.5, 49, 49, 51.25, 51.25) cm
19 (19, 19½, 19½, 20½, 20½) inches

#12 is sleeve cuff width
24.5 (24.5, 26.75, 26.75, 29, 29) cm
9¾ (9¾, 10¾, 10¾, 11½, 11½) inches

#13 is sleeve width at top
50 (50, 52.25, 52.25, 54.5, 54.5) cm
20 (20, 21, 21, 21¾, 21¾) inches

FINISHED MEASUREMENTS

Allowing approximately 5–10 cm (2–4 in) of ease.

	Bust		Base of neck to hem	
	Metric	**Imperial**	**Metric**	**Imperial**
S	96.75	38½	65.75	26¼
M	105.75	42½	65.75	26¼
L	116.75	46½	68.25	27¼
1X	125.75	50½	68.25	27¼
2X	136.75	54½	70.75	28¼
3X	147.5	59¼	70.75	28¼

YOU WILL NEED

8-ply (DK) yarn; I used Cleckheaton 'Country' 8-ply:

> 20 (22, 25, 26, 29, 31) 50 g (1 ¾ oz) balls

> or 1920 (2050, 2330 ,2465, 2780, 2955) metres

> or 2100 (2240, 2550, 2695, 3040, 3230) yards

approx. 60 g (2 oz) Himalaya Yarn 'Sari Silk' (see Resources)

5 mm (US8) needles

5 mm (USH) crochet hook (or hook or needles in size to suit the edging of your choice)

bead mix in colours to suit; I used red, clear, green, matte blue/purple mix, in sizes 11 and 8

Gauge: 18 sts x 24 rows over 10 cm (4 in) worked in st st

Notes

- The yarn for this garment was worked at a looser than standard gauge which allows for more drape in the fabric.
- Because the fabric is stocking stitch the edges of this garment will roll.
- Tip for shoulder cast-offs worked over several rows: When doing the 2nd and subsequent cast-offs, if you slip the first stitch in the group to be cast off this will make for a better slope to the shoulder, making it easier to create a better looking seam.

INSTRUCTIONS

BACK

Cast on 86 (94, 104, 112, 122, 132) sts. Work in st st (knit on RS, purl on WS) for 37.5 (37.5, 38.75, 38.75, 40, 40) cm or 15 (15, 15½, 15½, 16, 16) inches, ending with WS row.

Armhole shaping

Cast off 8 (8, 9, 9, 10, 10) sts at beginning of next 2 rows. Work even on 70 (78, 86, 94, 102, 112) sts until armhole measures 25 (25, 26.25, 26.25, 27.5, 27.5) cm or 10 (10, 10½, 10½, 11, 11) inches, ending with WS row.

Shape shoulders and back of neck

At the beginning of each of the next 5 rows, cast off 5 (6, 7, 8, 9, 10) sts, work to 13 (14, 14, 15, 16, 17) sts on needle and cast off the next 14 (14, 16, 16, 16, 18) sts at centre for back of neck, work to end of row, turn. Cast off 5 (6, 7, 8, 9, 10) sts and work to end of row, turn. Cast off 7 sts at neck edge, work to end of row. Cast off remaining 6 (7, 7, 8, 9, 10) sts. Attach yarn at beginning of centre cast-off sts, cast off 7 sts and work to end of row. Turn. Cast off 6 (7, 7, 8, 9, 10) sts.

LEFT FRONT

Cast on 44 (48, 53, 57, 62, 67) sts. Work in st st (knit on RS, purl on WS) to same length as back to underarm, ending with WS row.

Shape armhole

Cast off 8 (8, 9, 9, 10, 10) sts and work to end of row.

Shape shoulder

Work even for 18 rows ending with RS row. Increase 1 st at beginning of row and work even to 62.5 (62.5, 65, 65, 67.5, 67.5) cm or 25 (25, 26, 26, 27, 27) inches, ending with WS row. At the beginning of each of the next 3 RS rows, cast off 5 (6, 7, 8, 9, 10) sts.

Next RS row, cast off 6 (7, 7, 8, 9, 10) sts.

Shape collar

At beg of the next WS row, decrease 1 st, work to 2 sts remaining and p2tog. Work 4 rows even.

*At beg of the next row (WS), inc 1 st, work to 2 sts remaining and p2tog.

Work 3 rows even*. Repeat from * to * a total of 5 times.

Work 3 rows even and at the end of next RS row, k2tog. Work 1 row even.

At the beginning of the next RS row, cast off 4 sts, work to end of row and work 1 row even.

Next row, cast off 5 sts, work to 2 sts remaining and k2tog.

Work 1 row even and cast off 2 sts at the beginning of next RS row. Work to end of row and cast off remaining sts.

Right front

Cast on 44 (48, 53, 57, 62, 67) sts. Work in st st (knit on RS, purl on WS) to same length as back to underarm, ending with RS row.

Shape armhole

Cast off 8 (8, 9, 9, 10, 10) sts, work to end of row.

Shape shoulder

Work even for 18 rows ending with WS row, increase 1 st at beginning of row and work even to 62.5 (62.5, 65, 65, 67.5, 67.5) cm or 25 (25, 26, 26, 27, 27) inches, ending with RS row. At the beginning of each of the next 3 WS rows, cast off 5 (6, 7, 8, 9, 10) sts. Next WS row, cast off 6 (7, 7, 8, 9, 10) sts.

Shape collar

At beg of next RS row, decrease 1 st, work to 2 sts remaining and k2tog. Work 4 rows even.

At beg of next row (RS), k2tog, work to end of row, increasing 1 st at end of row. Work 3 rows even.

Repeat from * to * a total of 5 times.

Work 3 rows even and at the end of next WS row, p2tog. Work 1 row even. At the beginning of the next WS row, cast off 4 sts, work to end of row and work 1 row even.

Next row, cast off 5 sts, work to 2 sts remaining and p2tog.

Work 1 row even and cast off 2 sts at the beginning of next WS row. Work to end of row and cast off remaining sts.

Sleeves

Cast on 44 (44, 48, 48, 52, 52) sts.

Work in st st even for 4 rows.

K1 st, increase 1 st in the next st, work to 2 sts from end of row, increase 1 st in next st, K1.

Repeat from * to * every 4th row 17 times more, and every 6th row 5 times to reach 90 (90, 94, 94, 98, 98) sts.

Work even until sleeve measures 47.5 (47.5, 49, 49, 51.25, 51.25) cm or 19 (19, 19½, 19½, 20½, 20½) inches from beginning. Cast off.

FINISHING

Block and steam garment pieces.

All seams unless otherwise indicated are sewn together, RS uppermost, using mattress stitch (see How To chapter).

Join front and back shoulder seams.

Match cast-off edge of sleeve to armhole edge of body, easing in any fullness, and sew together.

Sew seam joining front to back and underarm sleeve seam.

Join short edges of each collar at back seam, then join collar to back neck edge with WS held together, easing in fullness.

EDGING

You can proceed with your own edging if you prefer or knit 4 rows of moss stitch on each edge.

If you don't have circular needles or don't like using them, you can join the shoulders and then work the armhole edgings of your choice before sewing the underarm seams together.

DECORATION

Weave Sari Silk along the junction where stocking stitch meets moss stitch on garment fronts. (Optional: Oversew each of the garment edges with Sari Silk using whip stitch.)

Fold back the collar and weave lengths of Sari Silk through the fabric until completely covered. Stitch beads randomly amongst the woven Sari Silk. How many beads you add will depend on whether or not you want a heavily encrusted collar.

Jade top

Before starting this project, please refer to 'A word about options …' at the beginning of the project chapter.

FINISHED MEASUREMENTS
Allowing approximately 5–10 cm (2–4 in) of ease.

	Bust		Base of neck to hem	
	Metric	Imperial	Metric	Imperial
S	95.5	38	64	24¾
M	104.5	42	64	24 ¾
L	115.5	46	70	27
1X	124.5	50	70	27
2X	135.5	54	76	28¼
3X	146.5	58 ½	76	29¼

Fig 135a

Fig 135b

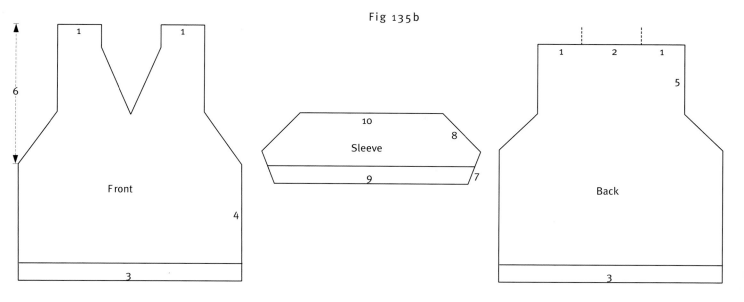

#1 is shoulder width for back and front shoulders
8.5 (10.5, 11, 13.25, 14.5, 17.25) cm
3¼ (4¼, 4½, 5¼, 5¾, 6¾) inches

2 is back neck width
10 (10, 11.75, 11.75, 13.25, 13.25) cm
4 (4, 4¾, 4¾, 5¼, 5¼) inches

#3 is bottom width of back and front
47.75 (52.25, 57.75, 62.25, 67.75, 73.25) cm
19 (21, 23, 25, 27, 29¼) inches

#4 is total length from bottom to underarm
37.5 (37.5, 40, 40, 42.5, 42.5) cm
15 (15, 16, 16, 17, 17) inches

5 is armhole depth for back
21.75 (21.75, 25.5, 25.5, 28.25, 28.25) cm
8¾ (8¾, 10¼, 10¼, 11¼, 11¼) inches

#6 is armhole depth for front
26.75 (26.75, 30.5, 30.5, 33.25, 33.25) cm
10¾ (10¾, 12¼, 12¼, 13¼, 13¼) inches

#7 is sleeve length to underarm
10 cm or 4 inches

#8 is sleeve cap height
9.25 (9.25, 10, 10, 10.75, 10.75) cm
3¾ (3¾, 4¼, 4¼, 4¼, 4¼) inches

#9 is sleeve width at bottom edge
47.75 (50, 52.25, 54.5, 56.75, 59) cm
19 (20, 21, 21¾, 22¾, 23½) inches

#10 is sleeve width at top
30 (32.25, 32.25, 34.5, 35.5, 37.75) cm
12 (13, 13, 13¾, 14¼, 15) inches

YOU WILL NEED

8-ply (DK) yarn; I used Cleckheaton's 'Country' 8-ply:

> 9 (9, 11, 12, 14, 15) 50 G (1 ¾ oz) balls

> or 780 (855, 1010, 1080, 1260, 1360) metres

> or 855 (935, 1100, 1180, 1380, 1485) yards

V-shaped overlay similar to the one in the photograph (if you can't find something similar you may like to add a few rows of rib to the neckline)

5 mm (US8) knitting needles

bead mix to complement colour of project

Gauge: 18 sts x 24 rows over 10 cm (4 in) in st st.

Notes

- The yarn is worked at a looser than standard gauge which allows for more drape in the fabric.
- The front is worked 5 cm (2 in) longer than the back to allow for the back of the neck shaping. Please note assembly instructions carefully.

Special instructions for armhole decrease shaping:

Row 1: Decrease 1 st at the beginning and end of the row.

Row 2: Repeat row 1.

Row 3: Repeat row 1.

Row 4: Work 1 row even.

Rows 5 and 6: Repeat row 1.

Row 7: Repeat row 4.

Rows 8 and 9: Repeat row 1.

Row 10: Repeat row 4.

INSTRUCTIONS

BACK

Cast on 86 (94, 104, 112, 122, 132) sts. Starting on RS, work ribbing (k1, p1) for 12 rows. Change to st st (knit 1 row, purl 1 row) to 37.5 (37.5, 40, 40, 42.5, 42.5) cm or 15 (15, 16, 16, 17, 17) inches from beginning, ending with a WS row.

Armhole shaping and shoulders

Continue in st st, shape armhole by repeating 'Armhole decrease shaping' of Rows 1 to 10 for a total of 22 (22, 25, 25, 26, 26) rows, to reach 54 (62, 68, 76, 84, 94) sts remaining.

Work even until armhole measures 12.5 (12.5, 15, 15, 17.5, 17.5) cm or 5 (5, 6, 6, 7, 7) inches above completion of the armhole decreases. Cast off all sts.

FRONT

Work as for back through completion of 'Armhole decrease shaping', ending with WS row. Next row, work 26 (30, 33, 37, 41, 46) sts, bind off centre 2 st and work to end of row. Working on Right Front only, work 3 rows even.

Next row, decrease 1 st at neck edge, work 2 rows even and repeat decrease on next row, next work 3 rows even.

Repeat from * to * for a total of 11 (11, 13, 13, 15, 15) decreases to reach 15 (19, 20, 24, 26, 31) sts. Work even to 17.5 (17.5, 20, 20, 22.5, 22.5) cm or 7 (7, 8, 8, 9, 9) inches above completion of the armhole decreases. Cast off all stitches. Join the yarn at the start of the 2-stitch centre cast off and work Left Front as for Right Front, reversing all shaping. Cast off all sts.

SLEEVES

Cast on 86 (90, 94, 98, 102, 106) sts. Starting on RS, work ribbing (k1, p1) for 12 rows. Change to st st (knit 1 row, purl 1 row) to approximately 10 cm (4 in), ending with a WS row.

Shape sleeve cap

Continue in st st, shaping the armhole by repeating 'Armhole decrease shaping' of Rows 1 to 10 as per back for a total of 22 (22, 25, 25, 26, 26) rows to reach 54 (58, 58, 62, 64, 68) sts remaining. Cast off all sts.

FINISHING

Block and steam garment pieces.

Using mattress stitch (see How To chapter), sew shoulder seams and mark the point on front armhole 2.5 cm (1 in) forward of the shoulder seam. This point should be matched to the centre of the sleeve cast-off to allow for the back neck to fit properly.

Sew sleeves to the armhole of the body.

Sew underarm seams.

DECORATING

If you are using an overlay which has been worked onto a net background, you will need to trim the outside edge of the net as close as you can to the stitching.

On the inside edge leave about 2 cm (½ in) of net; this will be folded over the inside edge of the neckline.

Fold the net extension to the inside of the neck and pin in place.

Sew overlay to the neckline using a small running stitch.

Stitch beads to outer and inner edges of overlay as shown in the photograph.

Walnut vest with wild trim

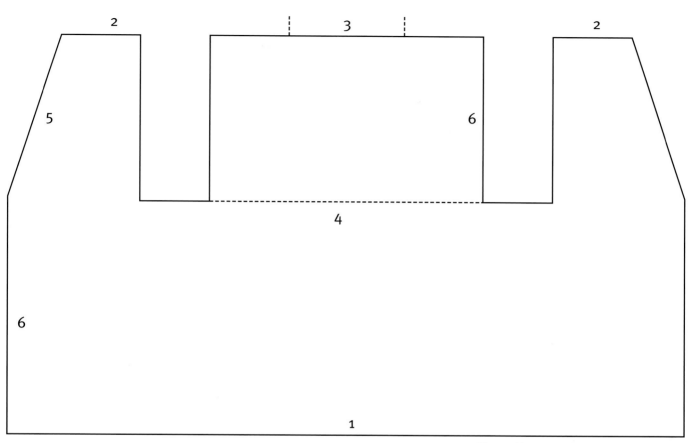

Fig 136b

#1 is bottom width
92 (102, 112, 122, 132, 142) cm
37 (41, 45, 49, 53, 57) inches

#2 is shoulder width for each front and back
9.25 (11.5, 12.25, 14.25, 15, 16.5)cm
3¾ (4½, 4¾, 5¾, 6, 6½) inches

#3 is back neck width
16.5 (17.75, 20.75, 22.25, 25, 27.75) cm
6½ (7¼, 8¼, 8¾, 10, 11¼) inches

#4 is width of the back from armhole to armhole
35 (40, 45, 50, 55, 60) cm
14 (16, 18, 20, 22, 24) inches

#5 is depth of armhole and 'V' neck
22.5 (25, 25, 25, 27.5, 27.5) cm
9 (10, 10, 10, 11, 11) inches

#6 is length of front edge from hem to start of 'V' neck shaping
27 (29, 31, 33, 35, 37) cm
10¾ (11½,12½,13¼, 14, 14¾) inches

Allowing approximately 5–10 cm (2–4 in) of ease.

	Metric	Imperial
S	91.5	36
M	102	40
L	112	44
1X	122	48¾
2X	132	52¾
3X	142	56¾

YOU WILL NEED

La Lana Wools 'Knitting Worsted':

4 (4, 5, 6, 7, 7) 113 g (4 oz) hanks

or 665 (800, 920, 1090, 1205, 1335) metres

or 730 (880, 1010, 1200, 1325, 1470) yards

1 skein La Lana Wools 'Jewels' (there will enough left over for at least one more item, such as Sue's hat, see page 117)

5.5 mm (I/9) crochet hook

Notes

- Garment is worked in one piece to armhole.
- *Gauge:* measured over 14 sts and 16 rows per 10 cm (4 in) worked in dc(sc).
- Special instruction for decreasing: insert hook into first st, pull yarn through, insert hook into next st, pull yarn through, then through all three loops on hook.

INSTRUCTIONS

Chain 124 (138, 152, 166, 180, 194) sts.

LOWER BODY SECTION

1st Row: 1 dc(sc) in 2nd ch from hook, dc(sc) to end, 1 ch, turn.

2nd Row: Work a row of dc(sc) increasing 1 st at each end of row, 1 ch, turn.

3rd Row: Work dc(sc) to end.

4th Row: As 2nd row.

5th Row: As 3rd row.

6th Row: As 2nd row.

7th Row: As 3rd row but ending with 4 ch to turn (counts as 1 tr[dc] and 1 ch sp).

8th Row: Miss first dc(sc), *1 tr(dc) in next dc(sc), 1 ch, miss 1 dc(sc), rep from * along row ending with 1 tr(dc) in last st, 1 ch, turn.

9th Row: dc(sc) in first tr(dc), *1 ch, dc in next tr(dc), rep from * to end, 4 ch, turn.

Rep last two rows until work measures 27 (29, 31, 33, 35, 37) cm or 10¾, 11½, 12½, 13½, 14, 14¾ in).

Next row: Work 1 dc(sc) in each tr(dc) and each ch sp to end, 1 ch, turn.

Divide for armhole
Work dc(sc) over next 25 (28, 32, 35, 39, 42) sts, 1 ch, turn.

Shape neckline
1st Row: Work in dc(sc) to last 2 sts, work dec, 1 ch, turn

2nd and 3rd Rows: Work in dc(sc) without shaping

Keeping armhole edge straight, continue working over these sts, decreasing 1 st at front edge only in every following 3rd row 6 (10, 4, 4, 2, 0) times, and every 2nd row 5 (1, 10, 10, 15, 18) times.

Work even to 22.5 (25, 25, 25, 27.5, 27.5) cm, or 9 (10, 10, 10, 11, 11) inches, until 13 (16, 17, 20, 21, 23) sts rem. Fasten off.

Join yarn to opposite edge and work dc(sc) over 25 (28, 32, 35, 39, 42) sts, 1 ch, turn.

Work as for other side, reversing shaping for front neck edge until same length. Fasten off.

BACK SECTION
Miss 15 sts for armhole, join in yarn to next st and work in rows of dc(sc)over the next 49 (57, 63, 71, 77, 85) sts until work measures the same as for front.

Fasten off.

FINISHING
Join shoulder seams using mattress stitch (see How to chapter).

TRIM
Stitch the trim to front and back neck edges as shown in the photograph.

Sorbet shrug

YOU WILL NEED

200 g (7 oz) Cleckheaton 'Country' 8-ply (Col A) for small size

NB: add 50 g (1¾ oz) yarn for medium size, 100 g (3½ oz) for large size

50 g (1¾ oz) ball Plymouth Yarns 'Gabrielle' (Col B)

5 mm (H/8) hook

optional beading:

> 5 pale green teardrop beads
>
> 8 red round beads, size 8
>
> 3 pink round beads, size 8
>
> 3 green round beads, size 8
>
> 10 bugle beads
>
> 5 seed beads

needle to fit through beads and beading thread

Fig 137a Front of Sorbet shrug

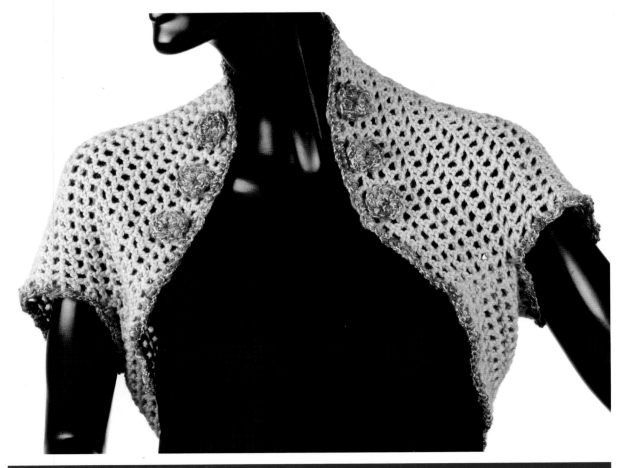

measured over filet mesh pattern – 17 sts [9 tr(dc) and 8 sps] and 9 rows per 10 cm (4 in).

Fig 137b Back of Sorbet shrug

INSTRUCTIONS

Sml	Med	Lge
Ch 111	(125,	139) plus 4 sts.

Note: For a larger garment add a block of 14sts plus 4 extra

1st Row: 1 tr(dc) in 5th ch from hook, *1 ch, miss 1 ch, 1 tr(dc) in next ch, rep from * to end.

2nd Row: 4 ch (counts as first tr[dc]), miss edge tr and first space, 1 tr(dc) in next tr(dc), 1 ch, miss 1 sp, 1 tr(dc) in next tr(dc) to end, working last tr(dc) in 4th ch of first 5 ch.

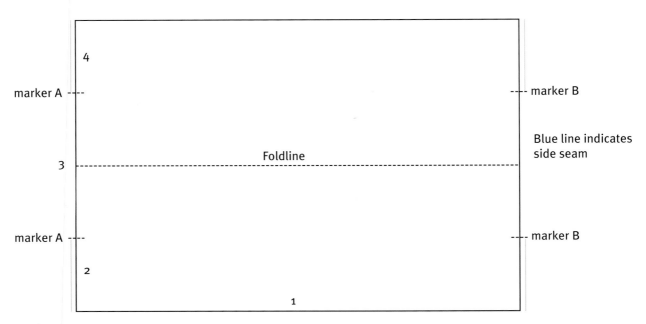

Fig 137c

#1 is Width of rectangle 65.25, 73.5, 76.5 cm 26, 29½, 30½ in	**# 3 is Length from 1st marker to 2nd marker** 30, 32.25, 34.5 sm 12, 13, 13¾ cm
#2 is Length to first marker 9, 10, 11 cm 3½, 4, 4½ in	**# 4 is Length from 2nd marker to edge** 9, 10, 11 cm 3½, 4, 4½ in

Rep 2nd row 6 (7, 8) times, working last tr(dc) in 3rd of 4 ch.

Place marker.

Work 27 (29, 31) rows for armhole.

Place marker.

Work 8 (9, 10) rows of mesh pattern. Fasten off.

Note: For a longer shrug you need to add extra rows before the first marker and after the second marker in sections marked with blue line.

FINISHING

Referring to Fig 137c, fold shrug in half. To form the side seam bring Marker A to other Marker A, and Marker B to other Marker B and sew from the marker to the edge.

TRIM

Using Col B, work a row of dc(sc) around armholes and lower edge of shrug.

Large circle

Make 4 ch, join with sl st to form circle.

1st Round: 3 ch, 11 tr(dc) into circle

2nd Round: 3 ch, 1 tr(dc) into same place as 3 ch, 2 tr(dc) in each st around circle.

3rd Round: 3 ch, 1 tr(dc) into same place as 3 ch, *1 tr(dc) in next st, 2 tr(dc) in next st, rep from * around circle, ending with 1 tr(dc) in last st. Fasten off, leaving a tail about 30 cm (12 in) long. Make one.

Medium circles

Work as for large circle, stopping after the 2nd round. Fasten off, leaving a long tail as before. Make two.

Small circles

Work as for large circles, stopping after the first round. Fasten off, leaving a long tail as before. Make six.

Stitch circles to shrug as indicated in the sample.

OPTIONAL BEAD FRINGE

Attach thread to centre of large circle. Thread on 2 bugles, 1 green, 1 pink, 1 red, 1 teardrop, 1 red, 1 seed bead. Miss the last bead threaded and take thread back up through all other beads. Secure thread at the top of this drop.

Move to next position and thread beads as follows: 2 bugles, 1 green, 1 red, 1 teardrop, 1 red, 1 seed bead—proceed as for first drop.

Move to next position and thread beads as follows: 2 bugles, 1 pink, 1 teardrop, 1 red, 1 seed bead—proceed as for first drop.

Repeat the last two drops on the other side of the centre drop.

Secure thread and fasten off.

HOW TO

CROSSING STITCHES

Note that the stitch pattern in the Textured Stitches chapter crosses 6 sts only. The process for 6 sts is the same as for 8 sts, which is shown below.

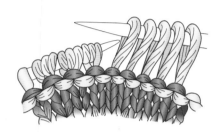

Fig 138a Slip the 8 lengthened sts onto the RH needle, dropping the extra loops

Fig 138b Place the first 4 stitches that were slipped back onto the LH needle, then the last 4 sts, thus crossing the first 4 over the last 4 sts.

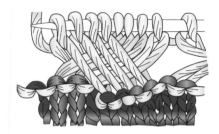

Fig 138c Knit these 8(6) sts in the order in which they appear on the LH needle, so that the 5th, 6th, 7th and 8th sts are knitted first and then the 1st, 2nd, 3rd and 4th sts.

TWISTED CORD

You can use different combinations of yarns to make these cords and they can be very effective for trims, handles or even neckpieces. If making handles you will need to ensure that the twist is tight.

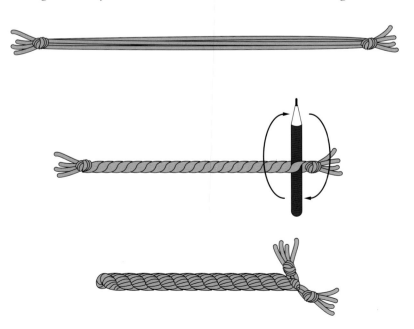

Fig 139

1   Take the required number of yarns and cut three times the length of the finished cord measurement. Knot each end.

2   Fasten one end of the cord around a door handle or slip it onto a pencil—it helps to work with a friend if you are using a pencil, but you can anchor it somewhere convenient if all else fails. Hold the strands taut and rotate in the same direction until the strands are tightly twisted. If the cord begins to kink up on itself rather than stay straight, you know you've twisted too much and you will need to untwist a little.

3   Fold in half at the centre and knot the ends together. Hold both ends and give the cord a sharp tug to even out the twist. You may need to smooth the cord from the knotted end to help this process. Tie a knot at the folded end and cut to make a tassel.

You can also use a special tool called a Spinster (see Resources) to make twisted cords, which makes the job even easier, or an electric drill at a very slow speed.

TASSEL FRINGING

ATTACHING A FRINGE

1   Cut multiple strands of yarn twice the length of the finished fringe. How many strands you use is dependent on how thick you want the fringe to be and on the thickness of the yarn you are using. Don't skimp on the amount used if you can help it, as a skimpy fringe will do nothing for your finished item.

2   Divide the strands into groups of 4 or more and fold them in half.

3   Using a crochet hook and with the WS of the work facing, draw the folded loops through the edge of the fabric.

4   Place all the ends over the hook, draw them through the loops on the hook, and pull up tightly.

5   Repeat evenly along the edge of the fabric.

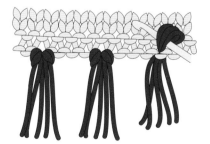 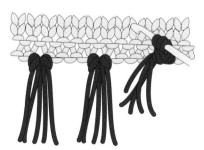

Fig 140

BEAD FRINGING

Bring needle and thread out of main piece where first fringe will be and thread on required number of beads plus one extra seed bead. Ignoring this last seed bead, go back up through all other beads and into the main fabric. Work a couple of tiny stitches at the top of this first drop, then work needle and thread along edge to next fringe position and repeat.

Fig 141

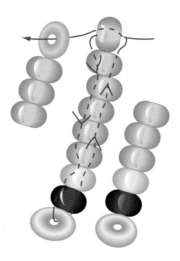

BEADED DOUBLE CROCHET (SINGLE CROCHET)

1st Row: Chain required number of stitches. Turn.

2nd Row: 1 ch, insert hook in 2nd ch from hook and draw yarn through, slide down bead or beads, yrh and draw through both loops. Cont to end of row. Turn.

3rd Row: 1 ch, work dc(sc) to end. Turn.

Repeat rows 2 and 3.

Fig 142

I-CORD

If you don't have a Wonder Knitter or Embellish-Knit tool as seen in the Toys of the Trade chapter you can make an I-cord as follows:

1   Using double-pointed needles, cast on 3 to 6 sts.

2   Knit all the stitches.

3   Without turning the work, switch the needles so the one with the stitches is in your left hand.

4   Slide the stitches to the RH end of the left needle. Pull the yarn gently to tighten it across the back of the stitches and knit the row again.

5   Continue in this manner until cord is the required length, cast off.

6   Gently tug the cord lengthways to help it form a nice shape.

STARTING A CROCHET CIRCLE WITH A LOOP

To start a circle without the use of chain stitches, form a circle (slip knot) as you would for beginning to crochet. Insert hook in normal position, but instead of tightening the loop, ch 1, and start single crocheting around the loop. You may need to pull the tail to tighten and draw the loop smaller as you work. Join with a slip st in first sc and pull the tail to tighten the loop.

Fig 143

BEAD HANDLES

For a 12 cm (5 in) diameter handle, you will need:

40 cm (16 in) heavy 16 gauge wire (or 20 gauge doubled and then
    twisted together) pliers

52 wooden beads size 10–12 mm

24 contrasting glass beads size 8 mm

Note: All beads need a hole large enough for the wire to go through. You can substitute the suggested beads for those of your choosing but you will need to adjust the quantity required to suit the desired length.

At one end of the wire make a small loop—this will prevent the beads falling off as you thread them.

Thread the beads onto the wire in the design of your choice for the length required for your handle.

Trim the ends to about 2.5 cm (1 in) and twist together once to secure. Wrap the ends several times around the join to finish. Don't worry that the join is showing between the beads as this will be hidden inside the handle carrier.

SHORT ROW KNITTING (SR)

Short row knitting is great for creating new shapes within your freeform work. It works in either stocking stitch or garter stitch.

To practise this technique, cast on 30 sts and work 4 rows.

Knit until 5 sts remain on your left needle. *Slip the next st in a p-wise direction to your right needle. Take yarn to other side of work and slip the stitch back onto left needle. Turn work and continue knitting to end of row.*

Knit until 7 sts remain on your left needle. Rep from * to *.

Knit until 9 sts remain on your left needle. Rep from * to *.

Holes are created by SR shaping. Look at your sample with RS facing and you will see a loop across the bottom of each of the stitches you previously slipped. To clean up the holes you need to knit that loop with its accompanying stitch as follows. (If you are knitting one row between each short row, as you work that one row stop before the stitch with the loop.)

Knit side facing: Pick up the loop and knit it with the stitch above it as shown in Fig 144. Continue to the end of the row.

Purl side facing: Pick up the loop and knit it with the stitch above it as shown in Fig 145. Continue to the end of the row.

Fig 144

Fig 145

Note: If you are knitting several rows between each short row, pick up the loop from below the slipped stitch on the first row worked after the short row, and then knit the rest of your row sequence.

Experiment with the way you work your short rows as you can achieve some fun results! Change the number of rows worked between each short row and play with the number of stitches worked before each short row turn.

SURFACE CHAIN STITCH

This stitch, also known as surface crochet, is commonly used for surface decoration, but it can also be used as a means of joining seams. The execution of the stitch is the same as when working surface decoration except that it is worked on the very edge of the fabric—see Fig 146.

With wrong sides together, join yarn to the work at the seam edge.

Hold working yarn behind fabric and insert hook from front through to the back. Pull yarn through fabric and the loop on the hook.

Insert hook into fabric again, pull yarn through fabric and then through the loop on the hook to complete another surface chain.

Repeat for length of seam.

When turning corners you will need to work 3 stitches into the same stitch in order to turn the corner smoothly.

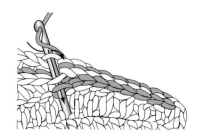

Fig 146 Surface chain stitch

MATTRESS STITCH

You work a mattress stitch seam with the right side of the work facing you. The technique works the same way whether it's knit or crochet fabric.

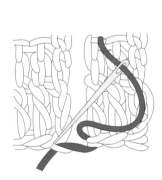

Fig 147 Step 1 Place the two pieces of fabric together, right sides up.

Fig 148 Step 2 Secure yarn to one side of the seam with 2 small stitches. Insert tapestry needle under the horizontal bar or loop between the 2 stitches.

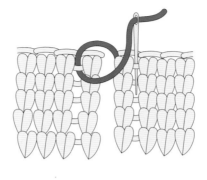
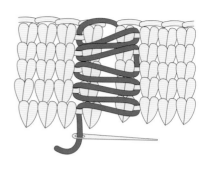

Fig 149 Step 3 Take yarn over to the other side and pick up a bar (knitting) or loop (crochet).

Fig 150 Step 4 Every 5 cm (2 in) or so pull yarn gently to close the seam. Continue alternating from one side to the other until seam is finished. Each time you close a section of the seam pull on both ends of the sewn fabric to help prevent puckering the fabric.

BEAD EMBROIDERY

STRAIGHT LINE BACK STITCH

Step 1 Use beading thread doubled with ends tied together in a knot.

Step 2 Pick up 3 beads and let them fall down to the fabric, positioning them into a straight line without any thread showing between the beads.

Step 3 Pass the needle through to the back of the fabric close up to the last bead.

Step 4 Bring needle up through to the front of the fabric between beads 1 and 2 and then through beads 2 and 3.

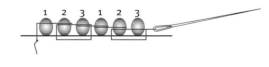

Fig 151a   Fig 151b

Repeat from Step 2 to Step 4 as required.

EMBROIDERY STITCHES

STRAIGHT STITCH

This stitch can is very effective worked as single stitches or grouped, overlapping, even or irregular, long or short. The stitches should lie flat on the surface and be neither loose nor pulled too tight.

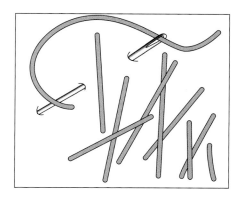

Fig 152a

Fig 152b

CHAIN STITCH

Bring needle up at 1 and insert at same place to form a loop.

Bring needle back up at 2, looping the thread beneath the needle as shown. Loop the thread under the needle as before and bring needle back up at 3.

Repeat as required to form a linked chain.

Fig 153

SEED STITCH

This stitch is generally used as a filling stitch and is made up of small straight stitches of equal length placed at random over the surface.

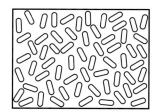

Fig 154

LAZY DAISY STITCH

Bring needle up through fabric at A, form a loop and hold it with your thumb.

Insert the needle back down through fabric at A and up at B.

Make a small anchor stitch to hold the loop in place.

Pull gently until loop lies smooth.

Lazy daisy stitch can be used in isolation or to make flowers.

Fig 155a and Fig 155b

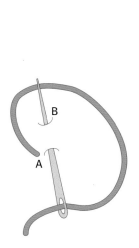
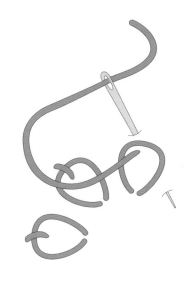

COUCHING STITCH

Hold a heavy thread or cord or several threads along the line to be followed.

Bring needle, threaded with finer thread or a contrasting heavier thread, up close to cord.

Take needle down on opposite side of cord to make a stitch at right angles to it.

Bring needle up to left in position for another right-angle stitch. Continue taking stitches over cord, spacing them evenly.

In freeform hand embroidery it's not strictly necessary to make precise right-angle stitches.

Other interesting effects may be achieved with couching stitch by working over several threads in (A) blanket stitch, (B) chain stitch and (C) feather stitch.

Fig 156

WHEEL

If you need to, draw around a cardboard circle of the required size with tailor's chalk or similar. Work anti-clockwise, turning the work as you go.

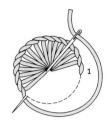

Bring needle up to edge of circle, down at the centre, up again a short distance along the edge with the thread beneath the needle as shown. Pull through gently. Repeat around circle.

Form the last stitch by passing needle under the first stitch at 1, and inserting needle at centre as before.

Fig 157

If you'd like a less formal 'wheel', move the insertion point off-centre.

Resources

Please join me at JennyDowde@yahoogroups.com
—a place where owners of my books can ask questions, get help, share their creativity and their freeform journeys with other like-minded people.

Cleckheaton Yarn
Australia
314 Albert Street, Brunswick, Vic 3056
email: enquiries@auspinners.com.au
http://www.cleckheaton.biz/

New Zealand
email: lynn@impactmg.co.nz

Plymouth Yarns (distributor of Cleckheaton Yarn)
All countries
http://www.plymouthyarn.com/

La Lana Wools
All countries
http://www.lalanawools.com/

Himalaya Yarn
All countries
http://www.himalayayarn.com/

Paillettes
All countries
http://www.trendsetteryarns.com/

Beads
Australia
http://www.uniquebeads.com.au/cgi-bin/beads.cgi?product=page2
For faux ivory and bone beads:
http://www.ozbeads.com.au/

Rhinestone and other decorative trims
Australia
Spotlight and Hobby Sew stores

United States
http://www.expointl.com/c-35-rhinestone-trims.aspx
This online store also has lots of other interesting trims.

Clever Country 4-ply cotton
Australia
http://www.crochetaustralia.com.au/prod1047.htm

Bag handles
Australia
Spotlight and Hobby Sew stores
Also http://www.thewoolshack.com/

Silk curls, wool tops/rovings and throwster's waste
Available from spinning and weaving suppliers.

Australia
http://www.glenoraweaving.com.au/
http://www.treetopscolours.com.au/

United States
http://www.treenwaysilks.com/treetops.html

Hairpin tool
Australia
http://www.crochetaustralia.com.au/

United States
www.clover-usa.com

Needlefelting needles
Australia
http://www.punchwithjudy.com.au/ or
www.woolbaa.com.au/

United States
http://www.clover-usa.com/cat.php?k=51303

Foam hat blocks
Australia
http://www.highlandfelting.com/

United States
http://www.hatshapers.com/

¾ in plastic O-rings
www.clover-usa.com
or try hardware shops for rubber O-rings

Bucilla Knitwit Loom
Australia
http://www.thewoolshack.com/
http://www.crochetaustralia.com.au/

United States
http://www.knitwit.com/index.html

Daisy wheels
Australia
Spotlight stores
Also http://www.crochetaustralia.com.au/

United States
http://lucettelady.50megs.com/
http://www.homesteadweaver.com/how-to-kits.htm
for various small weaving looms and lucets

Knitting looms, pom pom makers and other good stuff
Clover Wonder Knitter, Yo-Yo Maker and Pom Pom Maker

Australia
http://www.punchwithjudy.com.au/
This supplier also has hairpin tools as well as lots of other useful toys including size 11 beads on hanks (great for bead knitting and crochet), Big Eye needles, Shisha mirrors, tube turners, needles, hooks, etc.
http://www.thewoolshack.com/
Lots of good knitting supplies here including the Clover Pom-Pom Maker.

United States
http://www.clover-usa.com/

Embellish Knit (used to be called the Magi-cord)
http://www.bond-america.com/
http://www.waynesthisandthat.com/knittingnancys.html
An interesting site with information about various cord knitting tools.

Cushion inserts
Australia
http://www.goldiecushions.com.au/

Spinster™ Twisted Cord Maker (also known as a 'cord drill')
Australia
www.punchwithjudy.com.au
Phone: 02 6920 2238

United States
Do an online search for 'spinster cord maker', or ask your local craft stores.

Handmade paper
Australia
Peter Stanford, PO Box 2175, Normanhurst NSW 2076
email: bscheyb@optusnet.com.au

Gliftex software
www.ransen.com

Reading List

INSPIRATIONAL MAGAZINES

Australian Textile magazine: http://www.ggcreations.com.au/tafta/

Fiberarts magazine from Interweave Press: http://www.interweave.com/

Ornament magazine: http://www.ornamentmagazine.com/

Belle Armoire from Stampington Press:
   http://www.stampington.com/index.html

INSPIRATIONAL BOOKS

Jan Beaney and Jean Littlejohn, *Stitch Magic, Ideas and Interpretation*,
   B.T. Batsford, London, 1998, 1999, 2005.

Nancy Eha, *Bead Creative Art Quilts*, Creative Visions Press, Stillwater,
   MN, 2006

Katherine Shaughnessy, *The New Crewel: Exquisite Designs in
   Contemporary Embroidery*, Lark Books, Asheville, NC, 2005

Although these two books were written primarily for machine
embroiderers, as a non-embroiderer I found them to be full of
inspirational ideas that could be interpreted and used by knitters and
crocheters in other ways:

Valerie-Campbell-Harding, *Edges and Finishes in Machine Embroidery*,
   B.T. Batsford, London, 2004

Maggie Grey, *Raising the Surface with Machine Embroidery*, B.T. Batsford,
   London, 2003, 2004